D1190953

Curriculum Models
in
Adult Education

Curriculum Models
in
Adult Education

by
MICHAEL LANGENBACH, Ph.D.
University of Oklahoma

ROBERT E. KRIEGER PUBLISHING COMPANY
MALABAR, FLORIDA
1988

Original Edition   1988

Printed and Published by
ROBERT E. KRIEGER PUBLISHING COMPANY, INC.
KRIEGER DRIVE
MALABAR, FLORIDA   32950

LIBRARY OF CONGRESS
Library of Congress Cataloging-in-Publication Data

Langenbach, Michael.
  Curriculum models in adult education / by Michael Langenbach.
    p. cm.

  Bibliography: p.
  Includes index.
  1. Adult education—United States—Curricula—Planning.
I. Title.
LC5251.L33 1988   374′.973—dc19   87-26846
  ISBN 0–89874–984–0

10 9 8 7 6 5 4 3 2

To
Mary Ann, Amy, and Lisa

Contents

List of Figures

List of Tables

Preface

Knowledge of curriculum models and their development is important to adult educators because, unlike conventional, K-12 educators, the majority of adult educators actually develop curricula as a routine part of their jobs. The variety of purposes adult education serves and settings in which it occurs have given rise to a number of curriculum models, knowledge of which should provide the adult educator with greater flexibility in creating access to learning.

Many people come to study adult education as a field after having had some experience in it. Frequently this experience has been within a relatively narrow band of adult education practice. These practitioners may be well skilled in curriculum development within their sphere of specialization, but know little or nothing of curriculum models that are used in other areas of adult education. This book is intended for those who wish to know more about curriculum models and their development for a variety of adult education purposes.

Acknowledgments

Special thanks to Tillman Ragan who read the entire manuscript and offered insightful suggestions. Thanks also to Shirley Hodges, Liz Smith, and Robbie Hackler who patiently and effectively typed and retyped.

Introduction

Adult education is a developing field of study. It manifests itself in a wide variety of settings and takes such a multitude of forms that it defies facile description. Despite the lack of conceptual clarity, adult educators, like many professionals, make decisions that can have a profound effect on the lives of others. The professional literature is beginning to meet the challenge of providing resources for solving or at least analyzing the problems adult educators face. A notable exception is in the area of curriculum. There are some discussions of curriculum in terms of goals and objectives, activities for learners and instructors, and evaluation, but little attention has been paid to curriculum as a field within adult education. And even less attention has been paid to the variety of curriculum models employed by adult educators.

Discussions of adult education curriculum have been hampered by two problems: the great variety of settings considered adult education and the reluctance of many adult educators to discuss curriculum as a legitimate topic. The unwillingness to focus on curriculum may be explained by some adult educators' interest in disassociating themselves from conventional, K-12 schooling. Curriculum appears to them to be the exclusive domain of K-12 endeavors. It need not be. The legitimacy of a curricular perspective in adult education becomes apparent when considering Apple's (1979) contention that one of the primary concerns of curriculum as a field of study is the task of creating access to knowledge. If creating access to knowledge is what curriculum is about, and that idea is expanded to include assumptions, decisions, and activities necessary to creating access, adult educators should benefit from knowing more about curriculum. Insights about curriculum may be gained by studying it as it appears in myriad forms in adult education.

Models represent reality and can be used as guides in planning for the educational and training experiences of adults. Graphic models "enable planners to visualize curriculum components, their relationships, and the processes of development and implementation" (Zais, 1976, p. 93). Verbal constructs can be used in the same manner as graphic models. McClure claims, "a construct, whether it be the 'Tyler Rationale' or some other, gives curriculum planners the confidence to move forward and be creative" (1979, p. 146).

A curriculum model, then, is the plan that creates access to education and training. Most of the curriculum models described here will include the decisions and activities that are necessary for developing the actual curriculum. The model can be simple or complex. It must be general enough to be adaptable to different settings, but sufficiently specific to serve the purpose for which it was designed. The study of curriculum models can provide not only guidance in planning particular programs, but insight into the appropriateness of certain models for certain purposes.

Purpose

The purpose of this book is to describe several curriculum models that represent the diversity of the adult education field. The construct, curriculum model, will include what is commonly considered curriculum development.

The effort is introductory and inevitably incomplete. No attempt has been made to be exhaustive as in the manner of Sork and Buskey (1986), who reviewed ninety-three program planning models. Their work stands alone as an ambitious treatment of program planning in adult education. Instead, the present goal is to look more closely at a smaller number of models that, at least partially, represent the variety of purposes served by adult educators.

Criteria for Selection

Because there is such an array of adult education activities, the first step in making the complex picture manageable is to categorize according to some criteria. Two primary criteria emerged: clarity of purpose and sufficient detail of development or design. Examining the various purposes served by different adult educational activities appears to be a useful way to proceed. The sufficient detail criterion is necessary because only the original source will be used for description. No attempt will be made to analyze actual implementation.

The question of purpose, or more precisely, the conflicts associated with purpose, have been raised whenever education has been planned. Stubblefield (1981) claims the focus of adult education should be on life fulfillment while McGinnis (1981) argues for human liberation. Both emphases may be too broad to guide curriculum development. It appears, however, that if a single purpose could be decided upon, the process of curriculum development could proceed apace. Settling the question of purpose does permit focusing attention on appropriate means and the process by which they are determined. If the quest for a single, all-encompassing purpose for adult education is suspended and it is acknowledged that several different purposes are served, the process of curriculum development vis-á-vis different purposes can be examined.

The study of curriculum models then begins with establishing the purpose for which the models were developed. A classification of the purposes should facilitate the description of the models discussed in this text.

It is apparent, for example, that a Human Resource Development model for designing a training curriculum is embedded within organizations. The primary, if not exclusive, purpose of such a model is to increase the organizational effectiveness for its potential trainees. Vocational and technical educational programs serve business and industry, to be sure, but because most are undertaken before actual employment within an organization, the model for curriculum development will be less likely to serve a specific organization's needs, than the HRD model developed by Nadler (1982).

Adult education programs designed to promote a liberal education can take many forms but the Paideia Proposal (Adler, 1982) and the Great Books discussion group approaches are two of the most common. The Bachelor of Liberal Studies program offered through the Continuing Education and Public Service division of the University of Oklahoma and the American Library Association's "Let's Talk About It" programs are two other curriculum models designed to create access to a liberal education.

Educational programs intended to aid oppressed people by improving their literacy skills and/or their political awareness and effectiveness have been developed in contexts different from those out of which programs for continuing professional education have grown. Curriculum models for literacy training are likely to be different from models to enhance the skills, say, of practicing nurses.

Single purpose models describe a large portion of adult education, but do not account for enough. Many adult educational activities do not fit cleanly within a single purpose category. This does not mean, however, that they have not refined a curriculum development model appropriate to their many purposes. Perhaps the largest, formalized system of adult education—the cooperative extension service—is one example of a multipurpose adult education enterprise. Beal et al. (1966) have developed such a multipurpose model.

By far the most frequently occurring adult education is self-directed learning. Both Tough (1979) and Knowles (1975) have developed patterns or models from their research and experience that will provide an interesting comparison to the more formalized curriculum models. Whereas curriculum models deal with creating access to education and training, self-directed models address gaining access. Comparing the efforts to create access with efforts to gain access should be helpful to those responsible for curriculum development.

Finally, two general purpose models purport to have greater applicability than any of the above. Houle's (1972) *Design of Education* and Boone's (1985) conceptual programming model have been promoted as appropriate for a wide variety of purposes. Each of these generic models will be described.

The particular models selected for examination met two criteria. One criterion was to be reflective of a primary purpose. Unfortunately, the descriptions of curriculum models are not always so straightforward regarding purpose, hence a certain amount of ambiguity creeps in quickly. Some single purpose curriculum models do exist, but many are multipurpose or proposed as generic, forcing some arbitrary classifications in order to proceed.

The second criterion for selection was sufficient attention to development activities that precede the curriculum or sufficient detail to the design of the curriculum itself, in order to permit an understanding of the process or its product. A danger regarding criteria is to assume one model is preeminent and judge all others as being more or less like it and defining, perhaps unwittingly, the ideal model.

A curriculum can be characterized as reflecting a liberal, progressive, behaviorist, humanist, radical, or analytical philosophy of education (Elias and Merriam, 1980). There could be some profit in classifying curricula according to their philosophical underpinnings. The philosophical approach will be only touched upon within the descriptions because while some models clearly exhibit relatively pure philosophical positions, e.g., the competency-based as behaviorist and the liberal education as liberal, other models blur philosophical lines of demarcation.

In contrast to beginning with philosophy, perhaps the most abstract level at which to describe a curriculum, the beginning point here will be purpose, which is more likely to be consciously avowed and more easily detected than an underlying philosophy. Choosing purpose as an organizing construct is not without its conceptual problems. Indeed, the purpose construct becomes fuzzy when models purport to be multipurpose or generic. Nonetheless, purpose is assumed here to be less abstract than philosophical foundation. Purpose is more likely to be evidenced throughout the various elements of a model.

Persistent Problems

Writers in curriculum and adult education have discussed several problems that warrant mentioning; because the problems are so frequently encountered in the professional literature and persistently plague educators who must make decisions about curriculum development.

One of the most common problems is differentiating between education and training. Education typically is conceived as having a humanistic base and making a significant change in self-concept and understanding. The ultimate example of education may be illustrated by Henry Miller's reaction to reading Bergson's *Creative Evolution*:

> Everything which once I thought I had understood crumbled, and I was left with a clean slate. . . . Everything which the brain has labored for a lifetime to assimilate, categorize and synthesize has to be taken apart and reordered. Moving day for the soul! (1961, pp. 215–216)

Education then would include changes in the way the world is viewed and changes in attitude, neither of which would necessarily be measurable. It follows, too, that educational changes cannot be predicted.

Training, on the other hand, is usually thought to be behaviorally based with an emphasis on change in observable performance of a skill. Compared with education, which becomes a part of the learner's being and is integrated by the learner, training oftentimes is superficial, and almost always specified in detailed terms of objectives. Training objectives, because of their behavioristic base, are more easily measurable. Because they are measurable, some educators believe the only way to demonstrate accountability is to place a premium on objectives that can be measured. If educational objectives are, by definition, nonquantifiable, there is a danger that training objectives may take precedence in a curriculum because they can be measured.

But the distinctions between education and training are not always clear, especially in the minds of learners. It may be that the curriculum models that place heavy emphasis on specific, behavioral objectives ought to be considered as training models and those that appear to give short shrift to such objectives ought to be considered education models. But it is not that simple. Even the most behavioristic models will be seen to at least attempt to accommodate educational objectives in deference to the observation that learners typically have both education and training motives in mind. Finally, only the most parochial behaviorist would deny the importance of objectives that are not amenable to measurement. It should be noted, of course, as Brookfield (1986) has observed, that some torturous efforts have been made to translate humanistic goals into behavioral objectives.

Another persistent problem is revealed in the principles or definitions that pertain to adult education generally. The issue concerns the degree to which adults voluntarily undertake an educational experience. Brookfield and Houle both incorporate "learning freely undertaken" as a principle (Brookfield, 1986, pp. 9–10) or part of a definition (Houle, 1972, p. 138) of adult education. If adult education means only those activities that are entered into voluntarily, what will the majority of training experiences be considered? Is the assumption of "learning freely undertaken" excluding a vast amount of education by virtue of it not being freely undertaken? When considering education or training for organizational effectiveness, whether it is called human resources development (HRD) or simply staff development or the mandated continuing education present in many professional fields, does not the assumption of voluntary participation become negated?

Perhaps the widely held idea that adult learners should be actively involved in helping to determine educational plans (curricula) is in deference to the obvious, but seldom mentioned fact, that many adults would rather not be developed, no matter whose idea it is. Negotiating between educator and learner appears to be a reasonable strategy in reconciling different needs and expectations. Some of the curriculum models specifically address the importance of achieving mutually agreed upon ends through mutually agreed upon means. The very relationship between educator and learner, however, is the essence of another persistent problem associated with adult education curricula.

Adult educators must make choices regarding the needs of learners. Brookfield (1986) presents a lucid discussion of this problem. The extremes are providing a cafeteria style response to learners' expressed needs, i.e., simply serving as a resource at the beck and call of the learner, to the imposing of a predetermined set of beliefs on the learner, in the manner of an evangelist. The middle road between these two extremes, according to Brookfield, is "to challenge learners with alternative ways of interpreting their experience and to present to them ideas and behaviors that can cause them to examine critically their values, ways of acting, and the assumptions by which they live" (1986, p. 23).

The final persistent problem to be mentioned here is more of a macroconsideration of a curriculum and its effects on people. Curriculum, and the entire enterprise of education, have been characterized by some as being primarily one or the other in the following pairs of opposites:

conservative or radical
classical or romantic (Jarvis, 1985)
a collection of courses or integrated (Jarvis, 1985)
pedagogical or andragogical (Knowles, 1975)
being from above or of equals (Jarvis, 1985)
a reproduction of K-12 schooling or a transformation of it (Griffin, 1983)
domesticating or liberating (Friere, 1970)
operational or intrinsic (Brookfield, 1986)

Collectively, the pairs are perfect examples of divergent problems that cannot be solved by the application of a rational problem solving method. The solutions to any or all of these divergent problems lie in the actual living through and experiencing them (Schumacker, 1973).

Whether any of the models described in the following sections clearly fall in any of the above categories is left to the reader's judgment. The characterization of a curriculum model as being one of the extremes of a pair may be useful in describing that curriculum's elements. The most important aspect of such characterization, however, is the statement it makes about the context out of which a particular curriculum is developed (Giroux, 1983).

Conventional, K-12 schooling has been convincingly argued by some to be virtually consistent with the social and political structures it represents (Giroux, 1983). The dominant paradigm Apps (1985) refers to, and the hegemony Apple (1979) discusses not only affect a curriculum, the way one independent entity can have an impact on another independent entity, they also have a pervasive influence on the conception, development, implementation, and evaluation of a curriculum. Nowhere is this more evident than in the institutional model of curriculum development.

Brookfield (1986) considers the institutional model too inflexible to accommodate the variety of purposes and goals embraced by adult educators. Joyce (1971) fifteen years earlier, advocated creating new "partial" institutions to break away from the institutional model that had been (and still is) too bureaucratic to effectively respond to human needs.

All of the curriculum models described in this book are not institution-bound. A few are individual or cooperative enterprises and several are variations of the institutional model, which means they may suffer from the built-in constraints that being associated with an institution creates. Other models are broader and include entire social systems or subsystems, while some can operate independently of any institution.

None of the persistent problems is isolated. The challenge will be to understand not just what decisions and actions are necessary for developing a curriculum, but discerning the underlying assumptions and values that serve as a springboard for both.

Organization

The descriptions of the curriculum models will highlight the purposes they serve, their goals and objectives, content, and the methods of instruction and evaluation they promote. These elements of a curriculum do not always receive equal treatment in the original developer's description. Some models include detailed descriptions of the development of each of these elements, but others are treated lightly. It is important to note that these elements have been considered as curricular commonplaces (Goodlad, 1979) and do not constitute any kind of ideal model, against which all others will be compared.

The persistent problems briefly mentioned above permeate all of the models. Discussion of some of the obvious intersections of problems with the elements of a model will follow each model's description in a commentary section. Comparisons and contrasts with other models also will be included in the commentary. Other facets, for example, the amount and kind of control educators and learners can exercise within a model, should be evident in its description.

This attempt is inspired in part by the efforts of others to conceptualize the field of adult education. Boyd and Apps' (1980) paradigmatic approach, Peters' (1980) systems approach and Schroeder's (1980) typology of decision control orientations are noteworthy efforts to make some order out of the "creative anarchy" that characterizes adult education. The approach used here will be to describe the various curriculum models and, when appropriate, their development in adult education. The models that are primarily single purpose will be described first, followed by those that are multipurpose, self-directed, and finally, generic.

SECTION I

ORGANIZATIONAL EFFECTIVENESS

Many different purposes are served by many different adult educational activities and many activities appear to serve several purposes simultaneously. The training that occurs within an organization, however, typically has but one overriding purpose: organizational effectiveness. The design and development of programs (or curricula) to enhance current employees' effectiveness have been important concerns within the field of human resource development (Nadler, 1984).

The Critical Events Model (CEM), developed by Nadler (1982), represents well all of the necessary (critical) events that should occur when planning training that will enhance organizational effectiveness. Although just one of the eight events of the model is called "Build Curriculum," the entire model will be considered a curriculum development enterprise. The model begins with determining needs, proceeds through objectives, content, strategies, and evaluation, all of which have been considered by many to be legitimate curriculum concerns.

Chapter 2 will address organizational effectiveness in a more general sense. The emphasis will be preparation for jobs, but the preparation will precede employment. Many vocational-technical schools prepare students through the use of competency-based training models. A generic competency-based model will be seen to be similar to, but not exactly the same as, the Critical Events Model. An important distinction is the setting in which the training takes place. In the CEM, the training is secondary to other organizational goals of profit or service. Vocational-technical schools, however, are considered institutions where training is the primary, if not exclusive, goal.

CHAPTER 1

The Critical Events Model*

The Critical Events Model (CEM) (Nadler, 1982) is made up of a series of events that should take place in order to design a training program. The CEM is "essentially based on training for jobs within a specified organization" (Nadler, 1982, p. xii).

The CEM is an open, as opposed to closed model. It is subject to change as conditions within or outside the organization change. It is not a mathematical model, nor is it predictive. The openness is in deference to organizations as well as individuals being very complex. Nadler states that "it is not possible to identify and determine all the variables when a program is being designed. Indeed the actual work of designing the program will probably bring to light practices and policies that have either been forgotten, overlooked, or are in the organization culture category" (pp. 11 & 13).

Figure 1.1 presents the model. As the figure depicts there are eight linear events and one common to all. The common event is Evaluation and Feedback. It is actually a component of each of the other events, once an organizational need has been determined. Evaluation and feedback are integral parts of identifying the needs of the organization and therefore not separated from that event. A brief description of each event will be provided to help the reader better understand the total model.

---

*For a more detailed description of this model, see Nadler, L. (1982). Unless otherwise indicated, all references in this chapter are to this source.

Identify the Needs of the Organization

The first event in the model should remind the reader the model has been designed for use within an organization and specifically within what Darkenwald and Merriam (1982) consider a noneducational organization, wherein the education or training is secondary and supportive of other goals. Using Darkenwald and Merriam's (1982) categories of aims, one can see that the CEM is appropriate for achieving the aim of organizational effectiveness.

It seems only natural, then that the first step in the process is to identify the organizational need. Within private organizations, the need most likely will be related to increasing profits, whereas in government or nonprofit organizations the need will be related to en-

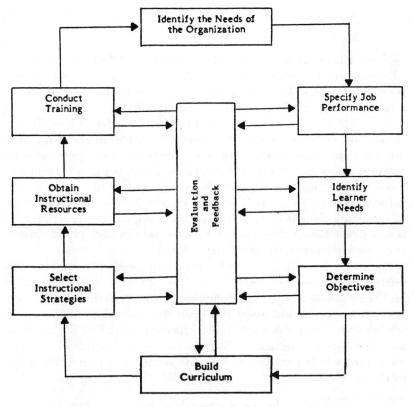

Figure 1.1   *The Critical Events Model (Nadler, 1982, p. 12).*

hancing service to the public. An organizational need could be created with the advent of new equipment (e.g., microcomputers or robotics), new government regulations (e.g., safety devices in automobiles) or interest in improving products (profit) or service.

Once a need is identified and agreed to by those people affected by it, alternatives should be considered before a decision is made to continue designing a training program to satisfy the need. A number of nontraining actions can be taken that could resolve the need.

Nadler suggests the people who are doing the work could be released and replaced to satisfy the need. The job itself could be redesigned or equipment could be changed without training. Finally, an organization change may produce positive effects in workers, sufficient to diminish the need. If the alternatives to training are neither possible nor sufficient, and the relevant parties are committed to establishing a training program, one can proceed to the next event.

Specify Job Performance

Job means "the work done by anybody in the organization from the lowest to the highest level" (p. 49). The job in question is one that has been identified as relating to the need of the organization. The need indicates, according to Nadler "the job is not being performed the way somebody (or some group) in the organization thinks it should be performed" (p. 47). It is important that agreement be reached regarding the role of the job within the organization and its specific performance requirements.

Specifying job performance is not as straightforward an endeavor as it may appear. One of the difficulties associated with this event is that of dealing with people's perceptions. It is complicated by the confusion of "what is" with "what should be" when people report their perceptions. Despite this inherent problem, one must proceed with other considerations within this event.

The nature of jobs. The job undoubtedly is related to other jobs within the organization. Nadler depicts this interdependency as an input/output relationship. The job in question receives input (which was another job's output), acts on the material or information, that is, performs the job, and produces output, which in time may become another job's input. One needs to consider the input side of the job in question. The materials, supplies, data, whatever constitutes input, may not be up to standards for the job to be performed. The output is assumed to be below standards, or there would not have been a need in the first place.

Sources of information. A prime source of information would be the person or persons actually doing the job. It may be that the person performing the job would like to change it and sees the inquiry about the job as an opportunity to suggest how it should be changed. This is to be expected and the difference between what the performer does and would like to do needs to be noted.

Another source would be peers. Those people who are doing similar jobs within or even outside the organization may provide information about the job that the actual worker may miss.

Supervisors or managers should be consulted in order to understand their perceptions of the job. Indeed, they may be the first source because, in many instances, they may have been the ones who initiated the idea that training was needed.

One also could consult professionals who teach or conduct research about the kind of job in question. Many universities have faculty members who could provide useful information about job performance.

Written documents may contain relevant information about specific job performance. Production records and performance appraisals should provide background information regarding criteria or standards of performance. Financial statements also may indicate expectations of performance. Official job descriptions, though possibly dated, should address in general terms the performance expected for the job.

Methods of obtaining information. One needs to consider several variables associated with efficient data collection procedures and the possible impact the procedures can have on the people from whom the data are being collected. Nadler discusses several aspects relating to questionnaries and interviews. One must keep in mind that the objective during this event is to obtain information that helps to specify exactly what the job performance is.

Economy of time and effort can be achieved by calling a meeting of relevant parties for the express purpose of collectively determining job performance. It is not practical, in most situations, to have all relevant sources in attendance, and meetings where supervisors and subordinates are present may stifle some participants.

The most direct method of gathering job information is to observe the job being performed. The focus should be on the job, however, not on the individual performing it. Before any observation, the supervisor, as well as the subordinate, should be apprised of the purpose and use of the observation. One should realize too that performance of the job can be affected by awareness of being observed.

Finally, one could ask the job performer to keep a log of important aspects of the job. A log or recorder could be useful in capturing verbal snapshots of crucial elements of the job.

Evaluation and feedback. With regard to specifying job performance, the collected data should be transformed into easily communicated information that can be shared with others. Nadler suggests the potential learners be included in the information sharing along with supervisors and managers. Interdependent job holders might be included, but numbers may dictate otherwise. The most economical method of sharing is a meeting of relevant personnel. The meeting size needs to be kept manageable, hence, including interdependent job holders may not be advisable.

More than one meeting may be required in order to reach consensus on the information. At the final meeting it is imperative the following decisions be made:

1. Is there still agreement on the problem (or needs)? . . .
2. Is there agreement on job performance? . . .
3. Should consideration be given to alternatives (to training)? . . .
4. Will time be allocated for training (pp. 79–80)?

When the participants reach consensus on the above questions and training still seems to be indicated, one can proceed to the next event.

Identify Learner Needs

In the previous event it was determined what constituted specific job performance. In this event the focus is on the individual and the intention is to identify gaps that separate the individual from performing according to the specifics agreed upon earlier.

Before describing the steps in needs analysis, it should be noted that not all performance deficits are instances of learning needs. For example, it may be that values are keeping a person from performing up to standard. Nadler cites examples from sales where "selling up" may be expected as part of the job, but resisted by the salesperson as being too "pushy." It is wise to consider whether or not a person's values are preventing optimum performance. If it is a matter of values, either training will have to address those values or transferring the person to another job may be indicated.

Needs. The CEM uses needs that are directly related to job performance. Other needs, sometimes called wants or interests, are not within the purview of the CEM. It is clear that identifying learning needs cannot be accomplished without first determining organizational needs (Event #1) and specifying job performance (Event #2).

Sources of information. The primary source of information about learning needs is the person(s) actually doing the job. Nadler emphasizes the importance of the preceding event when he states:

> When going to the employee as the source, the Designer will automatically be verifying if the employee knows what is expected in job performance (Event #2). . . . If the employee had been involved (in Event #2), this statement of job performance will not be new (p. 92).

If a new process or product is affecting the job performance, the employee may not feel threatened by lack of performance. If, however, the gap between job performance and employee performance is not attributable to a new process or product, the employee may become hostile and negative. Nadler stress the necessity of being skilled in interpersonal relationships when dealing with this potential hostility and negativism.

The supervisor is another important source of information. Nadler observes that the supervisor is the one who most often will have requested the training.

Performance appraisals should contain relevant information regarding an employee's performance. Unfortunately, practice has shown that written appraisals are not reliable sources.

Finally, production or output records may provide help in determining learning needs. There is the possibility that records are not kept and that employees have no knowledge of criteria for adequate production. In such cases, the supervisors would require training rather than the job holders.

Methods of obtaining information. The methods in this event are similar to those of the previous event, but the focus here is on the learning needs of those people doing the job for which the training is being planned. Meetings would be an economical way to get information collected and shared, but involving supervisors and potential learners could mean work operations have to be halted. If all potential learners are not able to attend, representatives of the group should be present. Nadler warns that a stigma may be attached to such meetings in that they may be seen as being called for a group of losers. The negativism is not inevitable, however, especially if the meetings are short and focused on information from the previous event (expectations of job performance) and actual performance of job holders.

Potential trainees can be interviewed to obtain their perceptions of needs vis-á-vis job performance requirements obtained from the previous event. Again, it may not be possible to reach all employees, because of geographical location or other reasons. A representative sample will have to suffice when all employees are not available.

Observing potential learners on the job should provide usable information regarding learning needs. Nadler advises this procedure may indicate who needs training and who does not, thus reducing false expectations and saving training costs.

Questionnaires could help determine learning needs when personal contact is not possible. Questionnaires should be short and directly related to the job being performed.

Listing learning needs. Nadler suggests a "subtraction" method to determine needs. If one knows job performance (P), from the previous event and what the potential trainee currently knows or does (KD), from the current event, one can discover needs (N) by comparing P with KD, i.e., $P - KD = N$.

The results of the comparison should be listed as specifically as possible. Nadler cautions that care should be taken that the needs, as listed, communicate the same meanings to all the people involved.

Evaluation and feedback. Once the needs of learners have been identified, the list should be compared with the list gathered in the previous event (Specify Job Performance). If there is a discrepancy in the lists, one or both of the events will have to be reexamined. The point is that learning needs determined in the current event should be related to job performance.

The list of needs can be categorized for ease of communication. Needs probably will vary among individuals and Nadler advises showing, when possible, which individuals have specific needs.

The feedback should include the same people from whom data were obtained during this event. Nadler suggests some caution, however, with employees for whom the information may be too sensitive. Sharing the lists of needs with supervisors is imperative, but specific needs might be shared only with potential learners, thereby protecting the right of privacy of those concerned.

The following questions must be asked at this juncture:

1. If the needs are met, will job performance become accepted? . . .
2. If the needs are met, will the (original organizational) problem be solved? . . .
3. How important are the needs? . . .
4. Should the job be redesigned? . . .
5. Should tasks be reallocated? . . .
6. Should subordinates be transferred rather than trained? . . .
7. What is the availability of the learners (pp. 100–101)?

If the responses to the questions indicate training is still in order, the next event is begun.

Determine Objectives

"An objective is the statement of what is to be accomplished by an activity" (p. 105). Within this event two levels of objectives (general and specific) will be addressed: 1) with respect to a training program (general) and 2) learning experiences (specific).

The training program objectives must relate to the organizational and learning needs determined in earlier events. These needs should be listed according to their priority. Criteria for priority will vary, depending on the situation. Time, resources and the availability of personnel could collectively serve as criteria for ranking the needs. More likely, one of them will take precedence over the others and become the major criterion by which the needs are listed in priority order.

Factors external to the organization also can affect the priority of needs. Nadler states, "If the organization is under attack from consumer groups, government agencies, or competitors, the range of needs that can be satisfied would be different from a situation where there is no such attack" (p. 107).

After the needs are listed in terms of priorities, it may become apparent that all the needs cannot be met. Objectives will be written only for those that can be achieved within the training program being designed.

Types of objectives. Several different classification schemes exist for categorizing objectives. Nadler notes this and uses a three domain taxonomy: psychomotor (skill), cognitive (knowledge) and affective (attitude or value).

Skills are observable. They require practice to learn. Learning a skill means learning how to act or perform in some way. Compared with other types of objectives, skill objectives are relatively easy to write.

Knowledge cannot be as easily equated with performance. One can know something, but not act on it. If knowledge is required for a certain performance, it must be learned before the performance can be expected. Knowledge can be viewed as affecting the capacity for changing performance.

Attitudes are elusive. Typically attitudes are inferred states of mind or predispositions. Certain behaviors can reflect certain attitudes, and vice versa. There is disagreement about which precedes which, but attitudinal objectives should not be ignored simply because of the controversy surrounding their appropriate treatment.

Process of determining objectives. General program objectives should be determined with the collaboration of the relevant supervisors. They are the ones who will have to make the learners available for training and are directly concerned with the performance which will be affected by the training. Managers also could be involved in determining objectives. At the very least, the managers should be informed of the process and given the opportunity to review the objectives once they are written.

Nadler suggests involving the potential learners in this phase is optional. If the potential learners have been involved in the previous event(s), it may be redundant to involve them here.

Specific learning objectives are more focused statements of the general program objectives. Just how specific the objectives are ought to depend on the anticipated instruction. If some form of programmed learning—teaching machine or computer assisted instruction—is to be used, the objectives need to be as specific as possible. If a professional trainer will be the instructor, the objectives need to be general enough to provide latitude to the instructor.

Nadler advises the objectives be stated in terms of the desired outcomes and should not simply describe content or practice. The standard three components are:

- Performance
- Condition
- Critèrion

Performance is what the learner will be able to do at the end of the training. The performance should be observable and measurable whenever possible.

"The second component is *condition*, which specifies the limitations or constraints under which the performance is expected to take place" (p. 116). Time may be a factor included under condition.

The third component is *criterion*, which is the standard that will be used to judge acceptable performance. It may be that less than 100 percent can be acceptable for some jobs. The criterion should reflect a realistic expectation of effective performance and not just an ideal.

Nadler notes that establishing criteria that include both qualitative and quantitative elements will be more difficult for jobs that are less measurable, such as managerial and some service jobs. He also warns that some supervisors may not have ever established such criteria for jobs, much less, informed employees of them. When the criteria are set and employees informed, the need for training may not be as great as before, or it may be necessary to shift the focus of training to the supervisors regarding job assessment and communication skills.

Evaluation and feedback. The written objectives, both the general ones for the overall program and the specific, performance objectives for the actual training, should be shared with the supervisors and, if possible, with the managers and potential learners. The sharing gives all parties the opportunity to rethink the original organizational need (is it still an important need?) and examine the specific objectives for their relevance to improving job performance.

The learning needs, determined in the preceding event, should be rank-ordered and the appropriate objectives for each should be present. It may be that all the learning needs will not be met and that some of the objectives will not be achieved. The relevant parties should realize this as a result of the evaluation and feedback.

At the conclusion of this event, the supervisors, as well, possibly, as the managers and potential learners, will have opportunity to review, discuss and perhaps modify the general and specific objectives. Important questions to be answered in this event are:

1. Are the program objectives acceptable?
2. Are the learning objectives acceptable?
3. Have all the important needs been reflected in the objectives?
4. Is the priority of learning objectives acceptable?
5. Do the objectives relate to "Specify Job Performance"?
6. Can the objectives be met internally or externally (p. 122)?

Assuming the answers to the above questions suggest continuing an internal training program, the next event should be addressed.

Build Curriculum

Curriculum is loosely defined as a series of lesson plans. Each lesson plan will be headed by objectives, preferably written as skills, knowledge, and attitudes. The important consideration is that the objectives have corresponding content within the lesson plan. Before lesson plans are written, however, content must be selected, classified, and sequenced.

Variables to consider. The content of the curriculum, its selection and arrangement, will reflect assumptions about how adults learn. There are several learning theories from which to choose, but the field of learning theories is something of a quagmire, making a clean, easy selection almost impossible. Nadler reduces the choices to two: organismic and mechanistic.

The organismic theories are based "on the concept of the learning environment as a living and changing element. This does not mean that there is no form, but rather that it is a changing and constantly altering situation. The emphasis . . . is on process rather than product" (p. 127). On the other hand, "the mechanistic (learning) model is characterized by the stimulus-response approach. Learning is viewed as conditioning, with a strong emphasis on the quantification of the learning" (p. 127).

Another variable to be considered is the learner. Previous experiences with schooling or training may have a bearing on how the learner responds to the training being planned. Learning styles, e.g., visual, auditory, or kinesthetic may affect the selection, arrangement, and presentation of the subject matter.

The instructor will have an influence, as well. If the instruction will be mediated by a machine or computer, the skill and attitude objectives will have to be omitted. "If the instructor is a subject matter specialist, there is more latitude allowable in the curriculum than when the instructor is not as well versed in the subject matter" (p. 129).

One must decide whether to make the curriculum or buy one that already exists. General topics, such as maintenance, use of computers, and principles of leadership are available commercially, but may not fit exactly the needs and objectives that have been identified up to this point in the model. Costs may have to include not only outright purchase of materials, but other fees paid for subsequent use, reproduction of materials, or certified instructors.

Nadler suggests two possible compromises. One is to modify the purchased material to fit the needs and objectives. The other is to change the content for the derived objectives to agree with content from a purchased package. Judgment is required in either case and will have to be based on factors of cost, time, effectiveness, and political considerations.

Selecting and classifying content. Deciding what content is appropriate can be facilitated by the use of a subject matter specialist. This content specialist "should be able to provide input of specific content from which the Designer can select what he needs" (p. 132). The specialist may be found within the organization or outside it. College and university faculty members are a frequently used resource for subject matter specialists. Nadler suggests other sources for content specialists include trade and professional organizations and the Government Printing Office. Whatever the source, the content needs to be classified according to the following categories:

- Essential
- Helpful
- Peripheral
- Unrelated

Not all content is equal in achieving the purposes being pursued. Four questions will help to determine in what category content should be placed. The questions reflect the activities and decisions of the previous four events:

1. Will this content, if learned, meet the previously stated objectives?
2. Will this content, if learned, meet the previously identified needs?
3. Will this content, if learned, lead to the performance specified?
4. Will this content, if learned, solve the previously identified problem of the organization (pp. 136–137)?

The content for which all answers are positive should be placed in the Essential category. The categories can be filled in, at first, by the Designer, perhaps with the aid of the subject matter specialist, but eventually, the supervisors should be involved in corroborating the initial judgements. Nadler suggests many iterations may be necessary before everyone is satisfied with the assignment of content to appropriate categories.

After the content is selected and classified, decisions have to be made regarding the sequence. The sequence should reflect the content and assumptions about learning and the learners. For example, starting with the general and moving to specifics reflects a concern for the learner needing to see the whole or Gestalt first, before proceeding with specifics. Learning theories called Gestalt, field, or cognitive undergird the general to specific sequence.

Starting with specifics and moving to the general indicates a bias toward a behaviorist approach. Stimulus-response (S-R) or other kinds of conditioning techniques would be the appropriate theory base for the specific to general approach. When all learners are expected to have identical skill performances at the end of the learning activity, the emphasis on specifics, i.e., starting with them and using an S-R or operant conditioning method may be appropriate.

Other concerns for the learner include the need for social interaction (high or low) which, if high suggests starting with the general and proceeding to specifics. If low, effective use might be made of programmed instruction, where learners may not interact with one another at all.

Nadler lists other variations of sequence to include concrete to abstract, known to unknown, and observation to reasoning. "In each case, the reverse can be used as a content sequence" (p. 138). Nadler also advises, "Before starting to sequence, the Designer must have the content clearly stated and written. Sometimes the content itself will indicate the sequence, whereas at other times the learner will be the governing factor. Usually it is an accommodation to both" (pp. 138–39).

How the content is sequenced also can be affected by the delivery system intended for instruction. If all the learning will take place during one or more days, uninterrupted by work, the sequencing can be straightforward. If the learning sessions are interrupted by learners returning to work, the content will have to be broken into components that permit application, in small increments, on the job and encourage feedback to the instructor. The learning setting itself should permit trial without penalty in order to insure on-the-job effectiveness (where trial with penalty may preclude application).

Once content is determined, classified, and sequenced, the next step is to convert the material into lesson plans.

Lesson plans. Usually several lesson plans will be made from a curriculum. The lesson plan is organized in a manner that permits easy identification of objectives, preparation, time, content, instructor and learner activities and strategies. Lesson plans can be very detailed, for example, actual questions can be written out, or less detailed, giving the instructors latitude in their use of them. Professional instructors or instructors who have been trained for their use may not need the same amount of detail in the lesson plan as instructors with little training or experience.

Nadler advises there is no one best form for a lesson plan, but "it must reflect the interaction of content, sequence, type of instructor, type of learner, and the norms in the organization" (p. 145). The total time for the training will determine the number of lesson plans. If several days are involved, each day should have a lesson plan. If less than a day, lesson plans could be designed for each unit or segment, covering perhaps an hour's time each, or a half day each.

Nadler provides no space in his lesson plan format for evaluation, "because it is a pervasive activity that should take place at many points during each lesson" (p. 151). Formative evaluation occurs throughout the lesson, usually at the end of major topics. This evaluation is designed as feedback for the instructor. Formative evaluation may suggest the pace is too slow or too fast or that something may need to be cleared up before proceeding. Summative evaluation occurs at the end of the learning activity and provides information about how completely the objectives were accomplished.

Evaluation and feedback. By this time in the process two new documents have been produced: a curriculum that contains subject matter, classified according to importance, sequenced according to the order in which it will be presented, and some assumptions about the potential learners; and one or more lesson plans that contain specific information about objectives, preparation for the lesson, time, topics, and activities. Specification of instructional activities may be incomplete at this stage insomuch as the next event will include making final decisions about them. Nadler advises, "Bringing together the content, sequence, and assumptions about the learner (the application of learning theory) is extremely important. There must be a real congruency among these three elements" (p. 154).

If time allows, all the documents generated during this event could be shared with supervisors and managers. Including potential learners is optional at this stage, especially if they have been included in previous events. Time may not permit sharing all documents, thus requiring summarizing. Essential elements to share include "assumptions that have been made about the nature of the subject matter and the kinds of learners expected" (p. 154). If the assumptions are made explicit, the supervisors and managers will be able to compare them with their views of the learners. Ideally the views will correspond and the appropriate judgements can be made about proceeding.

Two other points should be addressed during this phase. One concerns time allotted for the training. Fairly accurate estimates of time should be possible at this stage and the feedback should indicate satisfaction or dissatisfaction with these estimates. Adjustments in content may have to be made if time required will be more than time allowed. The other point is the issue of "make or buy." Earlier in the event that decision was made tentatively. Now that content and specific lesson plans can be reviewed, the decision may be changed.

Questions that must be addressed at the conclusion of this event are:

1. Does the content meet the previously determined objectives? . . .
2. Will that content satisfy the identified needs of the learners? . . .
3. Does the content relate to performance? . . .
4. Does the content relate to the previously identified need of the organization? . . .
5. Is there agreement on the make-or-buy decision? . . .
6. Will potential learners be made available for the period indicated (pp. 156–7)?

If all the answers suggest continuing with the planning, the attention turns to selecting instructional strategies.

Select Instructional Strategies

Once the curriculum is complete in that it contains subject matter arranged in terms of its relative importance to the objectives and sequenced to indicate order of presentation, attention turns to selecting appropriate instructional strategies.

Nadler's use of the term instructional strategies encompasses "all the various teaching and learning activities as well as the supporting mechanisms that are used by all involved in the experience" (p. 162). Several factors must be considered when selecting an instructional strategy.

Nadler offers ten considerations of a bipolar nature that can affect the choice of strategy. For example, one may know beforehand whether the mode of instruction will be instructor centered or learner centered; individual or group; low instructor competence or high instructor competence; and low student motivation or high student motivation. Knowledge of any of these variables can help in choosing one strategy over another, but other factors also need to be considered.

Experts in the field of learning psychology may have recommendations for matching certain strategies with particular objectives. Nadler cautions, however, that single answers to complex problems, (and selecting instructional strategies is a complex problem), often mislead one into thinking other factors are not important.

Nadler considers the budget as being one of the most important factors and also the one most often overlooked when training programs are being planned. Some instructional strategies require the purchase or rental of equipment, the cost of which may not be absorbed by the organization. Cash flow problems can curtail the amount of latitude one may have in selecting strategies. Costs may be associated with facilities as well. Some approaches to instruction may require special room accommodations, e.g., TV monitors or several small rooms available for small group work and a larger room for the total group attendance.

The instructor may well have a bearing on what instructional strategies are chosen. If the instructor is a professional, it usually can be assumed that a wider range of strategies can be considered. Some professional instructors have preferences for certain strategies over others and, if this is so, the planning should take this into account. Training professional and nonprofessional instructors is another possibility, but will be discussed more in the next event of the model.

The learner must be considered in selecting instructional strategies. Some learners may be more comfortable with certain strategies than with others. Nadler advises this need not preclude the introduction of "new" strategies because "bridges" or warm-up exercises can be provided to help the learner become comfortable with the "new" technique.

After all of the above considerations are made the lesson plan is reexamined to see if selecting a particular strategy, or some combination of strategies, will have an impact on content or sequence. The appropriate changes in lesson plans are made when the instructional strategy is selected.

The instructional strategies Nadler identifies number ninety-six. His listing includes one sentence definitions and synonomous terms. Malasky (1984) provides a more detailed description of twenty-four of the ninety-six, adding suggestions regarding when to use, requirements, advantages and so on.

Evaluation and feedback. The analysis will include the instructional strategies chosen, the type of instructors required and highlights of what is readily available and what must be made, bought, or rented. The analysis of this event is provided for supervisors, possibly budget and finance managers, and the instructor, but not the learners. When the appropriate personnel have been given an opportunity to see the products of this event (summarized in an analysis), the following questions will have to be answered:

1. Do the instructional strategies complement the curriculum? . . .
2. If the lesson plans are implemented, will the objectives be met? . . .
3. Do the lesson plans reflect the identified learning needs? . . .
4. If the lesson plans are used, will they relate to current job performance? . . .
5. If the training is conducted using these lesson plans, will the (original organizational) problem be solved? . . .
6. Can the selected instructional strategies be implemented? . . .
7. Will the selected instructional resources be available when needed (pp. 182–183)?

Nadler emphasizes that question 4 specifically addresses current job performance. The time it takes to get to this event may have been sufficient to have changes occur at the job itself, e.g., new equipment or new supervision, thus rendering moot the intention of training to improve job performance.

Before actual training begins, one more preliminary event is necessary. Assuming all of the questions have been answered to indicate continuation, the next event, "Obtain Instructional Resources" must be accomplished.

Obtain Instructional Resources

In this event it is imperative that all the necessary resources will be made available. During this event the person (Nadler uses the term Designer) who has been the prinicpal actor throughout may step aside to have a manager type take responsibility for obtaining the necessary resources. This shift is more likely in large organizations where the designer is not viewed as part of management.

Nadler provides a checklist that will aid in planning this event:

Scheduling:
1. Are the necessary facilities available? . . .
2. Who will actually instruct? . . .
3. Will the instructors be available when needed? . . .

4. Do the instructors require training? . . .
5. Will the learners be available? . . .

Equipment and materials:

1. If to be purchased, is there a specific list of items? . . .
2. If to be produced in-house, is there a specific list of items? . . .
3. If to be rented, is there a specific list of times? . . .
4. For all equipment and materials, have delivery schedules been prepared? . . .

Budget:

1. Have there been previous budget estimates? . . .
2. What is included in the budget? . . .
3. Will the training be cost effective? . . .
4. Who will be charged for the training? . . .
5. Do you have alternative budgets (pp. 196–201)?

Evaluation and feedback. The analysis for feedback should include the lesson plans as back-up material, resources, budget, scheduling, selection of participants, and the identification and preparation of instructors. If it is determined that resources have to be cut, the impact of the cut should be described in terms of lesson plans that may have to be altered or eliminated and the consequent change in curriculum, objectives, and needs. All the previous events have an interrelationship and it is useful to remind managers that limiting the budget at this stage will have an impact on previously agreed upon decisions.

Financial personnel should be included in the evaluation and feedback because most often they will be controlling budgets within the organization. Managers are equally important to the process of decision making and ought to be included. Most important are the supervisors. They are the ones who ultimately judge the worth of the training insomuch as the training is designed to solve problems that probably were first identified by the supervisors. Involving supervisors is consistent with all the other events to this point.

The following questions need to be answered at the conclusion of this event:

1. Is the cost acceptable? . . .

2. Will the required physical resources be available when needed? . . .
3. Is there a list of potential learners? . . .
4. Can specific instructors be assigned? . . .
5. Will the training program, with modification, solve the problem (pp. 203–205)?

When the answers to the above questions suggest continuing, the final event is begun.

Conduct Training

Although some changes in the program may still be made during this event, it is assumed to be completely designed by this point. As indicated earlier, the one who designed the program may step aside here for a supervisor. In smaller operations the designer may perform the supervisory role, but the competencies required will be different.

The participants (potential learners) should have been identified by now. The supervisors are most likely to know who they are and the degree to which they need the planned training. Herein lies a problem alluded to earlier in the model. If the training appears to be punitive, the participants will not appreciate being singled out for it. Nadler suggests including as participants some who may not need the training, because their presence would help to offset any stigma that might be attached to participating.

However the participants are chosen, once identified, they should "know the objectives of the program and the criteria for being in the learning group. When sent by the supervisor, the participant should be able to focus on the problem that the training program is expected to solve" (p. 210).

The needs identified earlier, for which objectives were developed and content selected, should be verified before instruction begins. If the participants are the same who contributed their input to the earlier event, Identify Learning Needs, and significant job changes have not occurred, there should be no problem. If the participants are different or the job has changed the nature of the needs, the training should be suspended until the needs are verified as still being relevant.

Once the actual training begins it should be remembered that problems can arise. Consequently, some measures should be taken to anticipate problems before they occur and interfere with the program.

Nadler recommends having a back-up instructor who can take over if something were to prevent the original one from continuing.

Materials and equipment should be double checked to verify correctness and sufficient quantity. Having spare lamps for projectors and confidence that the instructor can make simple replacements of same are also good ideas.

As indicated earlier, evaluating the training takes place both during (formative) and at the end (summative). During the training the instructor will have opportunities to test (or at least receive informal feedback) to see if the intended learning is taking place. These opportunities should have been built into the lesson plans, occurring typically after major topics. Summative evaluation speaks to the effectivness of the overall learning intended by the training. Nadler cautions that the actual job performance improvement, or lack thereof, will be evaluated by the supervisor. The instructor measures learning only, but the testing ought to be as near to actual job requirements as is possible.

Evaluation and feedback. The analysis for this event may well be the only written record of the program that is retained. A brief history of the entire procedure (all the events of the model) may be appropriate. The most important analysis will address what the participants have learned. The summative evaluation results will be the basis for the analysis. If pretests were used, the comparison of pre- and post-tests could constitute the essential analysis.

All parts of the model, including the various aspects of each event, can be reviewed at this point and recommendations made for the future. In addition to the specific learning results, the evaluation can address efficacy of the model itself.

The analysis can be "shared as widely as company policy and individual privacy permit" (p. 224). If there are negative connotations for participants or supervisors, it might be advisable to limit distribution, especially if cooperation from those parties will be expected in the future.

The following questions need to be answered at the conclusion of this event:

1. Does it appear that the results of the program have solved the initial (organizational) problem? . . .
2. Is there a need to repeat the program? . . .
3. If the program is repeated, are modifications required (p. 225)?

Nadler recommends possible use of the Critical Events Model as a flowchart or condition board, and invites modification as conditions may warrant.

Commentary

The principle of analyzing a job and preparing learners to fit that job is the same principle espoused by Charters (1923) and Bobbitt (1924) when curriculum began to emerge as a field of study. Applying the principle within a specific organization and providing ample opportunities for evaluation and feedback eliminate the major drawback suffered by the earlier models, namely the lack of agreement on what constituted the "good life." Within the Critical Events Model the "good life" is organizational effectiveness.

Nadler's Critical Events Model (CEM) begins with an organizational need. The initial inquiry about the need is to determine whether a training program is an appropriate response. The model has been constructed for those instances when training will solve an organizational problem. The CEM is designed to enhance organizational effectiveness.

The model enables a logical, straightforward approach to designing a training experience that ultimately serves the need from which the process originally sprung. The model has a built-in validity check and openness in the form of the evaluation and feedback loop that is part of each event in the model. Continuous checking with supervisors and managers throughout the design process assures that the original organizational need(s) will be addressed. Potential learners are consulted as well, to help assure a good fit between training and trainees, but Nadler reminds us, "at this time we are only going to discuss those needs related to job performance. This is not to deprecate other needs that individuals have, but that is not the purpose of CEM" (p. 85). And in reference to assembling participants for a meeting he notes, "the Designer must realize that the work is being done for the supervisor and the organization and that the design process should not interfere with the work situation" (p. 99).

The CEM is an open model that is applied within a closed setting. The openness is evident through the evaluation and feedback process that is a concluding feature of each of the events. The information obtained from the evaluation and feedback can effect changes in the process and content up to that point. Continuation in the model is dependent upon reconciling the feedback with whatever progress has been achieved.

The overall setting is closed in that the organization is the universe in which the model operates. Use of the model is at the pleasure of the managers of the organization. The exclusive aim is to solve an organizational problem.

The CEM is especially designed for training, but Nadler suggests, with some modification the CEM can accommodate educational goals as well. It is important to note here, however, the specific definitions Nadler has for training, education and development,

> Training—learning related to the present job of the individual.
> Education—learning related to a future but defined job for which the individual is being prepared.
> Development—learning for the general growth of the individual and/or the organization (1982, p. 7 & Nadler, 1984).

The necessary modification of the CEM for education, as Nadler defines it, would include determining job performance from a job the employee currently does not hold. Learning needs would be more difficult, though not impossible, to determine.

The use of the CEM for development, which, in Nadler's use approaches what others consider education, is even more tenuous. The present or future job performance can be measured, usually quantitatively. The effectiveness of training and education programs can be assessed more readily than a development program because "development is *learning for growth of the individual but not related to a specific present or future job*" (Nadler, 1984, p. 122, emphasis in the original). The pervasive interest in the CEM for behavioral or performance objectives suggests major revision of the CEM to accommodate the relatively vague aims of development. Indeed, the model's integrity appears to be built upon the specification of job performance and learner needs vis-à-vis job performance. When a specific job is taken out of the picture, the appropriateness of the CEM is less clear.

Designers of educational programs (or, in Nadler's terms, programs for development) have struggled for centuries with the question of purpose or aim. That question of purpose or aim revolves around the values associated with "the good life" or some other ideal, as discussed earlier, in the Introduction. The CEM appears to require more agreement among parties for its effectiveness than has been achieved regarding some ideal.

When the purpose or aim is to improve organizational effectiveness, and the outcomes are new or improved skills, the Critical Events Model can be used to assure agreement throughout the planning process. Its openness accommodates the unpredictable aspects of human behavior, but its appropriateness in promoting something beyond a performance-based organizational effectiveness remains to be seen.

Another model that more closely resembles the Charters (1923) and Bobbitt (1924) approach in that it is not tied to a specific organization, but, like the CEM, is designed to improve general organizational effectiveness, is the generic competency-based training model used extensively by vocational-technical schools. A generic, compentency-based model will be described in the next chapter.

CHAPTER 2

The Vocational-Technical/Generic Competency-Based Training Model

The previous chapter contained a description of a human resource development (HRD) model for designing a training program *within* an organization. That model begins with the specific organization's needs and proceeds, from those needs, to develop a training program designed to satisfy the identified needs. This chapter will contain a description of a curriculum model that is driven less by a specific organization's needs and more by occupations and jobs. Because the driving forces are occupations and jobs, the model is considered generic, i.e., it is general enough to be used by many different kinds of organizations.

One of the most descriptive accounts of the generic competency-based model is Blank's *Handbook for Developing Competency-Based Training Programs* (1982). Blank's book will be the primary source for the description of the model that follows. Readers are encouraged to refer to it for more specific detail if needed. Page references will refer to it unless otherwise indicated.

The generic model is similar to Nadler's (1982) model in that both are designed to improve organizational effectiveness. Whereas use of Nadler's model almost always occurs within settings that are not educational in nature, Blank's generic model is designed primarily for educational and training organizations that prepare students for employment.

Before examining the actual model, it may be helpful to review briefly the context out of which the competency-based model evolved. The claims made for its efficacy are impressive when compared with the traditional vocational-technical training approaches used by organizations, agencies, and schools.

Blank (1982) claims two basic philosophies underpin the model. One is "the notion that human competence is the ability to actually *perform*. Knowledge, attitudes, and effort are of little value without results. The second philosophy— mastery learning—holds that most anyone can learn most anything well if given quality instruction and sufficient time" (p. vi, emphasis in the original).

The comparison between competency-based training and traditional training programs is made more clear by Blank in his effort to highlight essential differences. Table 2.1 contains four basic characteristics of the two approaches to training.

Blank suggests the most fundamental difference between the two is that the competency-based approach is very systematic. "Each component of a competency-based training program is designed, monitored, and adjusted with one thing in mind—results" (p. 4). Although

Characteristic	Competency-Based Programs	Traditional Programs
1. WHAT Students Learn	1. Are based solely on specific, precisely stated student outcomes (usually called competencies or tasks) that have been recently verified as being essential for successful employment in the occupation for which the student is being trained. These competencies are made available to all concerned and describe exactly what the student will be able to do upon completing the training program.	1. Are usually based on textbooks, reference material, course outlines or other sources removed from the occupation itself. Students rarely know exactly what they will learn in each successive part of the program. The program is usually built around chapters, units, blocks, and other segments that have little meaning within the occupation--instructors focus on "covering material."
2. HOW Students Learn	2. Provide trainees with high quality, carefully designed, student-centered learning activities, media and materials designed to help them master each task. Materials are organized so that each individual trainee can stop, slow down, speed up or repeat instruction as needed to learn effectively. An integral part of this instruction is periodic feedback throughout the learning process with opportunities for trainees to correct their performance as they go.	2. Rely primarily on the instructor to personally deliver most of the instruction through live demonstrations, lectures, discussions and other instructor-centered learning activities. Students have little control over the pace of instruction. Usually, little periodic feedback on progress is given.
3. WHEN Students Proceed from Task to Task	3. Provide each trainee with enough time (within reason) to fully master one task before being allowed or forced to move on to the next.	3. Usually require a group of students to spend the same amount of time on each unit of instruction. The group then moves on to the next unit after a fixed amount of time which may be too soon or not soon enough for many individual trainees.
4. IF Students Learned Each Task	4. Require each individual trainee to perform each task to a high level of proficiency in a joblike setting before receiving credit for attaining each task. Performance is compared to a preset, fixed standard.	4. Rely heavily on paper and pencil tests and each student's performance is usually compared to the group norm. Students are allowed (and usually forced) to move on to the next unit after only marginally mastering or even "failing" the current unit.

Table 2.1   *Basic Characteristics that Distinguish Between Competency-Based and Traditional Training Programs (Blank, 1982, p. 5)*

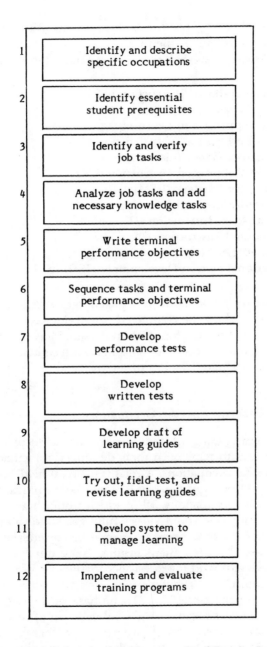

Figure 2.1   *Twelve Tasks to Develop a Competency-Based Training Program (Blank, 1982, p. 26).*

many labels have been applied to such programs, Blank believes the label is irrelevant as long as the program is a systematic approach to training. He lists several labels that have been used in the profession:

- Competency-Based Instruction (CBI)
- Mastery Learning
- Systems Approach to Learning
- Personalized System of Instruction (PSI)
- Performance-Based Instruction
- Criterion-Referenced Instruction (CRI)
- Learning for Mastery (LFM)
- Objective-Referenced Learning
- Individualized Instruction (II)
- Programmed Instruction (PI)
- Self-Paced Learning
- Instructional System Development (ISD) (p. 7).

The competency-based model is depicted in Figure 2-1. The model indicates twelve tasks to be completed in developing a competency-based curriculum. The first four tasks represent Phase One—describing the competent worker on-the-job; and the last eight tasks represent Phase Two—developing training programs.

Identify and Describe Specific Occupations

One of the shortcomings of traditional vocational-technical training programs appears to have been their designers' reluctance to offer training in specific occupations. A relatively broad field, such as auto mechanics, would be available, but it would be a program made up of several specific occupations, all of which would have to be taken and passed before one could successfully graduate. Students who stopped short of the total program, would be considered dropouts, and in some cases, failures. Blank argues, "since our trainees will be recruited, hired, and paid for *specific* occupations or jobs, that is how we should organize our training programs—not solely on *broad* occupational or program areas" (p. 31, emphasis in the original).

The ideal training program would be made up of several specific occupational titles within a broad program area, thereby creating an option for students to selectively enroll and stay enrolled in as many of the occupational programs as is desired or possible. Such a program is predicated on open entry and exit, where the emphasis is on mastering competencies and not just putting in the allotted time.

Sources for occupations. The most comprehensive source for occupational titles is the U.S. Labor Department's *Dictionary of Occupational Titles* (1977). It lists all recognized occupations and provides a description for each. Blank suggests several other sources for identifying occupations. These include an advisory committee that may be formed to provide assistance with decisions about program offerings; other employers, employees, labor unions and management within an occupational field; help-wanted advertisements; and other instructors.

The last step in identifying specific occupations is to subject each one to a set of criteria. The titles that satisfy all or most of the criteria are the ones that should be offered. Blank suggests the following criteria as examples:

1. Is formal training required for entry into the occupation?
2. Are we allowed or authorized by law, regulations, rules, or policies to offer training in the occupation?
3. Is reliable data available indicating present and future employment demand in the occupation?
4. Is there evidence that students are likely to enroll for training in the occupation?
5. Is the occupation at entry level and not a level of advancement for which workers are typically trained on the job?
6. Is the instructor(s) qualified and experienced in the occupation?
7. Is the facility, including tools, materials, and equipment, adequate or readily obtainable?
8. Would the demand for additional graduates be adequate to justify offering training in the occupation if other training programs exist nearby (p. 36)?

Job descriptions. Once specific occupations have been selected, job descriptions for each must be written. The *Dictionary of Occupational Titles* is a good source for job descriptions. Whatever the source, the job description should focus on the real world of work and not include anything about training. Typically, a job description will include information about general working conditions, equipment to be used, special abilities needed to work successfully, level of training required, and whether or not a license is needed.

Identify Essential Student Prerequisites

In order to assure a greater likelihood for success, Blank suggests identifying the necessary abilities and aptitudes. An example would be good eyesight for the occupation of drafting. Another might be average or above eye-hand coordination for an electrician. Making the prerequisites known will help counselors guide students and students self-select the training programs appropriate for them.

Identify and Verify Job Tasks

The generic model is based on job tasks successful workers perform on the job. Unlike traditional training and education, where other tasks, such as reading a textbook or enduring lectures, form the basis for training, the competency-based model is built around the actual tasks workers perform when they are employed.

Blank notes, "As we develop competency-based programs we should remember that competencies are those worthy accomplishments that make the employee *valuable to the employer* and that make the employer *valuable to the customer or consumer*" (p. 58, emphasis in the original). Determining what the tasks are is called occupational analysis.

The analysis of an occupation can be made from several vantages. One is to observe workers on the job; another is to meet with workers and collect the task information from them; and a third is to generate a tentative listing of tasks and submit it to workers for verification. Any combination of the above would satisfy this part of the model. Time and energy could be saved, however, by utilizing existing sources of analyses.

The Task Inventory Exchange, coordinated by the National Center for Research in Vocational Education, located at the Ohio State University; the V-TECS Consortium, comprised of several states and military branches, located in Atlanta, Georgia; and the DACUM Exchange, headquartered at Humber College, Ontario, are all useful resources to begin a listing of tasks for many different occupations. The initial listing will be tentative. The verification of the list, made by workers and employers selected to help in the process will be necessary before the job tasks identification step is considered complete.

Analyze Job Tasks and Add Necessary Knowledge Tasks

Occupations are made up of tasks and tasks are made up of steps and supporting knowledge and attitudes. Blank clarifies this procedure by stating, "Task analysis is the process of identifying and writing down the specific *skills, knowledges,* and *attitudes* that distinguish someone who performs a task *competently* from someone who *cannot perform* the task at all" (p. 94, emphasis in the original).

A task is fully analyzed, according to Blank, when there is a list of all the distinct, procedural steps, the facts, concepts, and other knowledges, and the critical values and attitudes that, when learned by students, will make them competent in that task at the trainee level. For instructional planning purposes it may be useful to consider each task as being made up of six major components

1. Actual steps in performing task from start to finish.
2. Technical knowledge needed to perform steps accurately.
3. Related math, science, or background information needed to understand or perform task competently.
4. Safety knowledge or skill.
5. Use of any special tools, equipment, and instruments needed to perform this particular task.
6. Attitudes critical to performing the task competently on the job (p. 94).

The technical knowledge needed to perform the steps of a task competently should be listed and ultimately learned with the tasks. Specific safety and attitudinal concerns, likewise, should be listed with the intent they be learned along with, as opposed to separate from, the tasks. Only those areas of knowledge, safety, and attitudes that apply to several tasks, and are therefore considered general, will be listed as separate competencies.

Analyzing knowledge tasks, i.e., identifying those areas of knowledge that need to be learned, takes the form of an outline. Unlike the step by step procedure in listing the performance tasks, the knowledge task analysis focuses on key points, facts, definitions, and abilities. The more precisely all of the above can be stated, the easier it will be to write specific objectives, the next task in the competency-based model.

Write Terminal Performance Objectives

The preceding four tasks of the competency-based model focused on the occupations in terms of identifying and selecting them, determining student prerequisites, and identifying job and knowledge tasks. Up to this point, the concern was with defining the competent worker on-the-job. From this point on, the concern shifts to developing a training program to prepare students for the job.

Writing a terminal performance objective (TPO) for each task will aid in the development of learning materials and tests. Blank defines a terminal performance objective as "a brief statement describing exactly what the trainee must do to show that the task has been mastered . . . (the TPO) describes the situation under which performance must be demonstrated, exactly what performance is required, and how well the trainee must perform to reach mastery" (p. 119).

Each task for the occupation needs to have a terminal performance objective. The TPO becomes the target toward which learning materials and experiences are aimed. TPOs also aid immensley in developing tests to assess mastery of the tasks. Each TPO should indicate what must be done, under what conditions, and how well for the student to be considered competent.

A number of sources contain already developed TPOs. Selecting and adapting, if necessary, from these sources will save time and energy. The V-TECS catalogs, ERIC documents (Educational Resources Information Center), textbooks, curriculum guides, and other instructors can be used as sources for TPOs. The important consideration is that each task has a TPO and that the TPO specifies the performance, conditions, and criteria for mastery.

Once an initial list of TPOs is completed, it should be verified by an advisory board or other consulting agent to see if the TPOs square with the "real" entry level competencies needed in an occupation. It is to be expected that the TPOs will be revised, according to expert suggestion and students' experiences with them.

Sequence Tasks and Terminal Performance Objectives

The traditional approach to sequencing tasks and performance objectives was to follow a text or instructor's outline, with little or no thought to the necessity of the particular sequence. In the model presented here the only requirement for sequencing tasks is to list any prerequisites. The point is to give students as much latitude as possible in determining the order in which they will learn a new task.

Whenever a certain task must be mastered before others are begun, a chart signifying the relative order of tasks can be constructed and displayed for students to see. The sequencing can be verified by an advisory group or by students who actually work through various sequences without undue difficulty.

Develop Performance Tests

The development of tests that assess mastery of tasks helps to assure that the competency being measured is competence in the task. That may appear simple-minded and obvious, but many traditional programs infer competency when students attend all sessions, read the text, and satisfy other, nontask related requirements. An essential element of compentency-based programs is that the tests are developed from the terminal performance objectives.

The TPOs form the basis of all the tests, and the TPOs are related to the original tasks of the occupation. The cycle is nearly complete, although the teaching/learning has not been addressed. More about teaching/learning later.

Blank notes four important uses of performance tests. The first is determining entry-level competence of students. Some students possibly could "test out" of some teaching/learning if they performed well enough. At the very least the students would have a relatively objective assessment of where they should begin their learning of the various tasks.

A second use of performance tests is the formative evaluation it provides students and the instructor as learning is taking place. The tests provide feedback to students that can help them adjust their approaches to the learning tasks accordingly.

A third use is assessing mastery. Oftentimes mastery of prerequisite tasks is overlooked and students struggle with subsequent tasks as a result. And certainly at the conclusion of training mastery must be assessed to assure competence in the tasks.

The fourth use of performance tests affects decisions made about the training itself: the materials, experiences, and the instructor. If students appear to be having too much difficulty passing the tests, the preparation leading up to the testing may be suspect.

Criterion- versus norm-referenced tests. A criterion-referenced test is one that has a predetermined criterion for passing. The standard for passing the test is based upon acceptable performance at the entry level in the occupation. A norm-referenced test is one that relies on a group's performance to determine an individual's score. The standard in a norm-referenced test is relative. The Blank model assumes the use of criterion-referenced tests exclusively. The idea of norm-referenced evaluation is antithetical to the competency-based emphasis of this model.

Process and product. The process within a test is how the student performs the task. The product is the end result. Blank notes, "Sometimes, *how* the task is performed is critical to attaining competence; other times, the finished *product* is what we are interested in, and in some cases we need to evaluate both process *and* product" (p. 166, emphasis in the original). Process items on a test come from the procedural steps within the task being evaluated. These steps were identified when the tasks were analyzed. The general rule to follow is to include process items only if they help to distinguish between someone who can perform the task competently and someone who cannot.

Product items ought to describe desirable characteristics of the completed product. Such characteristics could include size, shape, color, and/or condition.

The determination of a criterion for passing ought to relate to competent performance on the job. Blank claims anything less than 100 percent is not satisfactory. He admits this is a minority position, but asserts its legitimacy as long as only essential process and product-related items are included in the test.

Develop Written Tests

Performance tests are direct measures of task performance. Written tests "are used to assess a student's mastery of knowledge tasks and to assess mastery of complex or critical concepts or facts underlying skill tasks" (p. 179).

Of all the forms of written tests, Blank discusses only two: recall and recognition. He argues in favor of recognition types, most commonly found as multiple choice items. Obviously written tests can take many forms, and Blank simply states, whatever the form, they should measure only material directly related to the tasks and not anything judged to be extraneous.

The discussion regarding criterion referencing and 100 percent mastery as a standard that was made for performance tests applies as well to written tests. Once both types of tests are completed, attention can be paid to developing learning guides.

Develop Draft of Learning Guides

A learning guide is a package approach to training. The guide contains several components, each designed to help the student achieve the terminal performance objective for which the guide was developed. Learning guides are intended to be used by individual students, at their own pace.

According to Blank, the essential components of a learning guide are:

1. The *task statement* that tells exactly what will be learned;
2. The *introduction* that tells why the task is important. It serves, in a way, to motivate the student by addressing the question, Why should I learn this?
3. The *terminal performance objective* that specifies conditions, performance and standard of proficiency.
4. *Enabling objectives* that break the task down into smaller, more easily learned steps. They literally enable the student to proceed through to mastery of the entire task. Enabling objectives usually require the student to gain information from reading or other media, apply the information, and get feedback. With regard to the resources for information, Blank suggests, "the most appropriate resource to select or develop for presenting information for an enabling objective is one that is *effective* in presenting the skill or knowledge called for *and* the one that costs the *least* in time, money, and energy to purchase, develop and to use" (p. 230, emphasis in the original). Resources can be readings from a text, journal, or especially designed instruction sheet. Other resources include still pictures, slides, 8 or 16 mm films, audio and/or video-cassettes.
5. *Self-checks* that provide opportunities for students to test their learning as they proceed and obtain immediate feedback. Self-checks provide the formative (as opposed to summative) evaluation that can be of help to students and instructors. Self-checks can shed light on the effectiveness or appropriateness of the materials, instructions, and activities that have been used up to that point. The next section addresses the try out step for developing the learning guide.
6. *Written tests* that assess knowledge tasks.
7. *Performance tests* that assess actual performance of the original task for which the guide was developed.

Try Out, Field-Test, and Revise Learning Guides

Two phases of the tryout period are recommended. The first is to have one or two students go through the entire guide to see if it reads well and makes sense. The instructions need to be clear and references accurate and available. Whatever difficulties are encountered in this first phase should be corrected before phase two.

The next phase is the field test. From three to five students of average to above average ability should be selected for this phase. They should be students who would use the guide eventually; the guide should be presented as another, typical guide and not as something experimental that requires special attention. The students may work simultaneously on it or at different times, but not as a group.

After all the students complete the guide, they should be asked for their comments about it. Assuming no major difficulties were encountered as they proceeded through it, each should be asked how many hours it took to complete. The number of hours should be averaged to determine what will become a standard time for the guide. The standard time can be used for grading purposes discussed in the next section.

The students' comments and performance on the tests should speak to the appropriateness of the material and instructions used in the guide. Whatever changes are deemed necessary should be made and the guide should be put into use.

Develop System to Manage Learning

Whereas most of the managing in traditional programs is concerned with instruction, Blank claims management of competency-based, individualized programs is concerned with learning. It is particularly challenging when one realizes students can enter programs at various times, work on different tasks in different order, and progress at their own rates.

Blank suggests a management system be used that accounts for each student's plans and progress. Planning sheets can be completed when the student and instructor anticipate how much will be attempted over a certain period of time. Time cards can be used by students to keep track of the amount of time they spend on learning guides and record sheets can be used to keep track of tasks that are mastered. Official transcripts can be made from the verified record sheets for purposes required by employers.

Grades can be determined by comparing actual time spent on a learning guide with the guide's standard time, referred to above. If the two times are equal, the ratio would be converted to 100 percent. If more time is required, the ratio would be converted to a percentage that could represent A, B, C grades, if desired.

The physical environment may have to be rearranged to accommodate the emphasis on learning—which usually means room and facilities for students to carry out activities. Instead of the usual arrangement of instructor in the front and communication just one way, the new arrangement will have learning centers and stations where students can work on projects, both in the classroom and in the shop, and be able to move about as their activities require.

Logic and convenience should dictate what is located where. Noise, air pollution from running engines, and safety factors suggest certain activities occur in a shop area while others can be located within a classroom type of setting, but one with carrels and other designated spaces for reading, practicing, and testing.

Implement and Evaluate Training Programs

Exactly how one implements a competency-based program will depend on the nature of the program and the organization in which it will be used. Blank offers several guidelines that would apply to most programs and settings.

The overall concern is to be systematic in the approach taken. What needs to be done, by whom, when and how much it will cost should be determined before launching into the implementation.

The results-oriented emphasis of the model and how that differs dramatically from traditional training programs may be the first bit of information that needs to be transmitted. However, simply telling people about the "new" model will not work. Blank suggests practicing what is being preached.

If the setting is one in which traditional approaches to training are practiced, the challenge would be to have the current instructors motivated to learn about the competency-based approach. When that motivation is evident, a learning package can be provided for the instructors to work through, just as they, eventually, would be expected to provide learning packages for their students. Developing a competency-based package for instructors would involve the same steps followed in the model described herein. Tasks would have to be identified and listed, as well as essential knowledge and attitudes. Tasks, knowledge, and attitudes would have to be stated in the form of terminal performance objectives. Learning materials would have to be identified and collected. Finally, a learning guide would need to be written that would direct the "student" through the materials, provide self-checks and mastery tests.

The transition from a traditional approach to a competency-based one would have to account for gradual introduction of one and elimination of the other. That would mean the continuation of some approaches until all the materials for new versions could be assembled. Depending on the total program size, the implementation stage could take one or two years to accomplish.

Evaluation of the overall competency-based program should involve the process—how the program is working on a day-to-day basis, as well as the product—how well placed and trained are the former students. The process and product questions are similar to the efficiency and effectiveness concerns raised earlier. Efficiency speaks to obtaining the best results for the time, energy, and money expended. Effectiveness concerns the degree to which the process, whatever its efficiency, actually results in the desired product.

Specific questions dealing with process/product and efficiency/effectiveness can be found in Blank (1982, pp. 334–337).

Commentary

The vocational-technical/generic competency-based training model appears to accommodate the training needs of occupations where specific skills are necessary to perform specific tasks. Indeed, the specificity of tasks of an occupation is a prerequisite to developing a competency-based model.

It is probably safe to say the majority of vocational-technical training programs benefit from a competency-based curriculum. As long as specific tasks can be identified and agreed upon by those who know the occupations, a list of competencies can be determined and appropriate learning materials can be assembled. As was the case with the Critical Events Model, described in Chapter 1, the success of the model depends on the degree to which agreement can be reached regarding relevant tasks. With the CEM the agreement question was addressed at the end of every event; during the evaluation and feedback, and appropriate adjustments were made before proceeding with the next event. The competency model for vocational-technical training serves a larger, more diverse arena, i.e., many organizations; hence the evaluation and feedback would likely be less uniform regarding agreement or changes to be made. The competency-based model, like the CEM, is predicated on agreement of tasks and competencies.

The competency-based model is a straightforward, rational approach to curriculum development. The emphasis is on specific tasks—identifying them, determining competencies for each, and designing learning and testing materials to acquire and check for them. The model permits, in fact encourages, a learning emphasis, as opposed to a teaching emphasis found in conventional vocational-technical schools. Students can enter a program and, more important, exit, at their convenience.

Much of the model's integrity lies in its testing. Students can test out of parts of a program or the entire program by demonstrating their competence before engaging in any of the learning activities. Self-pacing and self-checking are characteristics that distinguish the competency-based model from others. The emphasis is on learners learning as opposed to teachers teaching.

Critics of the competency-based model could point to the difficulty in achieving agreement on any but the most rudimentary of tasks associated with an occupation. By trying to serve a variety of organizations, use of the model will likely involve compromises regarding some of the tasks considered essential.

The emphasis on tasks means an emphasis on history, i.e., the time lag between innovations in an occupation and inclusion in the curriculum could make some training outmoded until the new tasks could be incorporated. The emphasis on the past and usually the present, when possible, may preclude the future concerns of an occupation. The emphasis on specific tasks makes developing the curriculum a rational, step by step procedure. But if the objectives include non-behavioristic outcomes, the model is less useful. Training people to use judgment is not as straightforward as training them to use a jackhammer.

Finally, the competency-based model requires motivation to sustain one's progress through the learning package. Prospective welders may have that motivation (and reading ability) to see them through, but vocational-technical trainers, accustomed to conventional approaches to training, are not likely to be so motivated. Implementation of competency-based programs within a conventional setting may be the greatest challenge to its proponents.

When new or improved specific skills are needed by organizations and agreement can be reached regarding their identification, the critical events model or the competency-based model can be used. When, instead there is an interest in cultivating the intellect, i.e., providing a liberal education for adults, there is far less agreement and, consequently less specificity, on how to proceed. These limitations, however, have not prevented adult educators from building curriculum models to accommodate the goals of liberal education. Section II contains a description of four models designed to promote a liberal education.

SECTION II

LIBERAL EDUCATION

Whereas training for organizational effectiveness usually is involuntary, liberal education has to be voluntary. And whereas vocational training has an explicit ending point, liberal education terminates only when life itself does. According to Hutchins (1952) we cannot escape our responsibility for obtaining a liberal education:

> The liberal arts are not merely indispensable, they are unavoidable. Nobody can decide for himself whether he is going to be a human being. The only question open to him is whether he will be an ignorant, undeveloped one or one who has sought to reach the highest point he is capable of attaining. The question, in short, is whether he will be a poor liberal artist or a good one (p. 5).

One might blanch at the prospect of a lifetime of schooling to carry out the awesome responsibility of obtaining a liberal education, but the chief proponents (Robert Hutchins and Mortimer Adler) are equally emphatic that schools, as we know them, are not the places where liberal education occurs.

In the first place, both Hutchins and Adler insist the greatest obstacle to a liberal education is youth. They define a youth as anyone who has been in the uninterrupted care of an institution, including family and school. They concede that preparation for a liberal education can begin in school, but Adler advises:

Only through the trials of adult life, only with the range and experience that makes for maturity, can human beings become educated persons. The mature may not be as trainable as the immature, but they are more educable by virtue of their maturity (1982, p. 10).

Another way in which liberal education differs from organizational effectiveness is in the teacher–student roles. Training someone up to a certain, preconceived level of competence assumes the teacher, more times than not, is already at or beyond that level. Because liberal education is a lifelong endeavor, however, teacher and student are not always differentiated, nor are levels of competence as likely to be so specified. In the group discussion mode, for example, the effective leader or moderator, working toward liberal educational ends, is at most, the first among equals. The very questions with which learners interact frequently have no "right" answers, therefore, an expert, in terms of the liberal arts, is not at all like an expert in cell biology or welding. The model teacher of the liberal arts is also the model learner.

Finally, a good liberal artist is a generalist, not a specialist. People do specialize within the liberal arts, to be sure, but the idea of a liberally educated person is the ideal of a generalist: one who is comfortable with discussions of mathematics and science, history and philosophy, the social sciences and the fine arts.

A liberal education may be considered by some as a synonym for education. Probably every educational endeavor and many training activities contain a modicum of liberal education, but the selections included in this section promote liberal education as their raison d'etre. Chapter 3 contains a description of the Paideia program and the Great Books discussion group. Chapter 4 includes the University of Oklahoma's Bachelor of Liberal Studies degree program and the American Library Association's "Let's Talk About It" program.

The Paideia Proposal and Great Books Discussion Groups

The Paideia proposal and the Great Books discussion program share the goal of promoting liberal education. The means to the goal overlap, but differences can be explained by the preparatory nature of the Paideia proposal as contrasted with the "maturity" of discussion groups focusing on the Great Books.

The Paideia Proposal

Before proceeding with a description of the curriculum model associated with the Paideia (py-dee-a) proposal, it should be noted that the proposal was conceived and promoted for reforming schooling at the K-12 levels. Unlike most other K-12 proposals, however, the Paideia proposal is both simple and profound. It carries over to adult education the idea that education is lifelong. The Paideia proposal is considered basic education, but rudimentary skill development is only one part of it and is not isolated from the other parts. By basic, the proponents of the Paideia proposal mean preparatory to liberal education. A better understanding of the Great Books discussion groups will be possible once the outlines of a preparatory program for such discussions are delineated.

The roots of the Paideia proposal go back to John Dewey. Citing Dewey, Adler asserts that "the goal at which any phase of education, true to itself, should aim . . . is more education. Other objectives may surround that goal, but it is central" (1982, p.69). Eduard Lindeman, considered by many to be the first American philosopher of adult education, also reflects much of Dewey's influence. Although the Paideia proposal aims at preparation for adult education, its consistency with what it considers lifelong learning is unmistakable.

Adler advises, "to be truly educated is a state achieved by self-direction, usually long after schooling is completed, in the later years of life" (1982, p. 58). His concern with schooling, any type of formal education, is that "basic or advanced . . . [schooling] that does not prepare the individual for further learning has failed, no matter what else it succeeds in doing" (1982, p. II). Adler reinforces this connection later when he claims "self-education will be well or poorly done in proportion to the quality of schooling that prepares for it" (1983, p. 9).

The Paideia Model

The proponents of the Paideia proposal offer it as "not a detailed One Best Curriculum, but rather a set of principles, a framework, and a process" (Sizer, 1983, p. 109). The framework is depicted in Figure 3.1. Within the overarching purpose of liberal education, the three columns in Figure 3.1 represent different, more specific purposes. As will be seen in the description of each, the more specific purposes involve different roles for teachers and students, and somewhat different content.

Acquisition of organized knowledge. The first column of the Paideia model represents didactic instruction, or teaching as telling. The subject matter is the liberal arts: language, literature, and fine arts; mathematics and natural sciences; history, geography and social studies. These three areas "comprise the most fundamental branches of learning . . . [and] provide the learner with indispensable knowledge about nature and culture, the world in which we live, our social institutions, and ourselves" (Adler, 1982, p. 24).

Teaching by telling has to be the least effective way for a group of people to learn anything. Virtually all the indictments of any level of schooling, especially those made in the last twenty years, turn on the assumption that schooling means, with few exceptions, teaching by telling. The danger of didactic instruction is that it emphasizes the teacher's activity and not necessarily the students'. Adler warns about this danger and proclaims:

	Column One	Column Two	Column Three
Goals	Acquisition of organized knowledge	Development of intellectual skills - skills of learning	Enlarged understanding of ideas and values
	by means of	by means of	by means of
Means	Didactic instruction Lectures and responses Textbooks and	Coaching, exercises and supervised practice	Maieutic or Socratic questioning and active participation
	in three areas of subject-matter	in the operations of	in the
Areas Operations and Activities	Language, literature and the fine arts mathematics and natural science history, geography and social studies	Reading, writing speaking, listening calculating, problem-solving observing, measuring estimating exercising critical judgment	Discussion of books (not textbooks) and other works of art and involvement in artistic activities e.g. music, drama visual arts

The three columns do not correspond to separate courses, nor is one kind of teaching and learning necessarily confined to any one class.

Figure 3.1   *The Paideia Model (Adler, 1982, p. 23).*

The basic pedagogical precept of the Paideia Program is that all genuine learning arises from the activity of the learner's own mind. . . . When the activities performed by the teacher render students passive, the latter cease to be learners—memorizers perhaps, but not learners (1984, p. 47).

In order to initiate and maintain activity on the learner's part Adler (1984) has seven recommendations for didactic instruction:

1. Attract and sustain attention by expecting answers to questions after the lecture. No more than half a class period should be

spent on telling; the other half should be devoted to questions and answers.

2. Whenever possible teachers should demonstrate enthusiasm and imagination in their presentation.
3. Introduce wonder and discovery in the material; e.g., casting the lesson as a kind of puzzle with attendant pleasure of discovering the solution.
4. Avoid talking at a level beyond the grasp of students as well as talking down or being obvious and condescending. "The middle ground consists in telling students things they can readily understand side by side with things they must make some effort to understand, that effort being re-enacted in the question period after the talk" (p. 52).
5. Make the question and answer period after the talk a two-way process, i.e., students asking the teacher and the teacher asking students.
6. Prepare for good listening by introducing the order of the talk, present the main body, and then summarize. The more structure in a talk, up to the point of being stilted and dull, the more likely it will be understood.
7. Emphasize quality over quantity. High quality presentations and questions and answers that follow, are more important than "covering" larger amounts of material.

Didactic instruction includes both written and oral presentations. The seven recommendations above apply to oral presentations when written material is either not available or inappropriate. When written material is assigned, the oral presentation should be a "brief but clearly organized summary (say 15 minutes) detailing what the students should have learned from the books or other written material, followed by a longer session of questions and answers" (Adler, 1984, p. 54).

Development of intellectual skills—skills of learning. The second column of the Paideia model represents coaching, where a student learns, in mathematics, for example, about "observing, calculating, and about how to troubleshoot, how to identify errors and figure out what caused them. He is learning fundamentally, how to think—logically, resourcefully, and imaginatively" (Sizer, 1984, p. 35). The term coaching is used because the activities of teachers and students are most like athletic coaches and athletes. The sessions are in effect, tutorial, and when appropriate, the other students may observe. The teacher uses "an artful blend of information, challenge, drill and encouragement" (Sizer, 1984, p. 35).

Seven essential conditions for good coaching are discussed by Sizer (1984):

1. Teachers must know how each student "thinks, attacks a problem, confuses things, loses or does not lose heart" (p. 40). The one-to-one relationship is most easily achieved through written work, where the student "converses"with the teacher and the teacher responds, in writing, regarding analysis or critique of the written work. It may be appropriate at times to coach more than one student at a time, but only when the needs of those students are very similar.

2. "The material of coaching is the student's work, in which skill is displayed for the teacher to criticize" (p. 41). Many students will resist the pressure to reveal their work for criticism, but if influential peers can be persuaded to begin the give-and-take of coaching, most of the others will follow their lead.

3. Immediacy of feedback is critical. Teachers must be able to respond promptly (and thoroughly) to the student's work. If too much time passes the benefit of dialog between teacher and student is lost.

4. Teachers must tell the students why or how their work is wrong; not just that an answer is wrong. Helping the student to see the reason for the error is the critical element in coaching.

5. Different subjects at different levels may require different techniques of coaching. Beginning writing or mathematics probably will call for approaches different from those appropriate for advanced writing or mathematics.

6. Drill is necessary. It is also often painful and boring, but without the repetition, there is little assurance that students will develop the habits associated with intellectual skills.

7. Coaching requires small classes and a lot of time. Typical high school schedules with which teachers and students must contend preclude effective coaching.

Sizer (1984) maintains the central focus of coaching as a technique is the "students' *doing*—thinking and expressing the results of thought" (emphasis in the original, p. 46). The teacher acts as a coach, working one to one with students as they gain skill by way of critiqued experience.

Enlarged understanding of ideas and values. The third column of
the Paideia model represents maiuntic or Socratic questioning. Maieu-
tic is of Greek origin and associated with midwifery. "(Socrates) called
his method of teaching something like midwifery because he viewed
it as assisting the labor of his companions in giving birth to ideas"
(Adler & Van Doren, 1984, p. 16).

The setting for the Socratic method is the seminar. It is different
from didactic instruction and coaching in that its primary purpose is
"to bring out and then clarify the ideas and issues that are raised by
something that has been read or otherwise experienced jointly by the
leader and the students" (Adler & Van Doren, 1984, pp. 18–19). Many
times the questions will not have "right" answers, but instead require
reflection on values and beliefs.

Adler and Van Doren (1984) describe the task of the seminar leader
as threefold:

> . . . to ask a series of questions that define the discussion and give it direc-
> tion; to examine or query the answers by trying to draw out the reasons
> for them or the implications they have; and to engage the participants in
> two-way talk with one another when the views they have advanced appear
> to be in conflict (p. 23).

The majority of activities of teacher and students in the seminar are
different from those found in didactic and coaching sessions because
the purpose they serve is different. There are times, however, when
it may be appropriate to draw upon didactic and coaching techniques
in seminar settings. In fact no one column of the model is entirely
"pure" in terms of teacher and student activities.

The subject matter of the seminars represents a significant change
from the rest of the model, as well as from the rest of conventional
schooling. The intent is simple: have students read and respond to
the most fundamental and lively issues. Adler and Van Doren (1984)
are straightforward in how to accomplish the intent:

> The ideas and issues raised by good books are more permanent and more
> interesting than those that are raised by inferior books. In fact, the best
> books—great books, as they are called—raise the most fundamental and
> lively issues of all (p. 19).

Unlike didactic instruction, where textbooks are read and supplemented with teacher talk, or coaching, where the emphasis is on performing basic skills, the Socratic questioning in a seminar is over

imaginative literature—fiction, drama and poetry, and expository literature—science, history and philosophy.

The teacher's preparation for a two hour seminar session begins with a thorough reading of the material. Notes are made regarding statements, definitions, key points, and arguments. Questions are developed to help students understand the material. Typically no more than five questions are written that require reflection and interpretation of the material. The questions are "ordered so that the first opens up matters to be further explored by the second; the second leads to further explorations by the third question; and so on" (Adler and Van Doren, 1984, p. 27).

Adler and Van Doren (1984) describe a leader's role through an example of follow-up questioning:

> The leader should seldom be satisfied with the answers given. The leader must always ask, Why? or: Is that all you think is involved? Who can add an essential point? Is not the second part overstated? Is _____ the right word for _____ (p. 27)?

All of the questioning and exchange should be done without talking down to students or treating them "as most teachers do when addressing them in a class session" (Adler and Van Doren, 1984, p. 28).

> The [seminar] leader should be patient and polite in dealing with everyone around the table—as patient and polite as one is with guests at one's dinner table. The leader should set an example of intellectual etiquette that the participants may learn from and imitate (Adler and Van Doren, 1984, p. 28).

The setting, as implied above, should be such that participants (preferably, fewer than twenty) sit facing one another. The conventional classroom setting of the teacher in front of rows of students is not appropriate for conducting seminars.

The Paideia proposal, considered here as a curriculum model, includes directions for three kinds of teaching-learning situations: didactic, coaching, and Socratic. The situations have been described as pure types, but overlap of methods and content is not unexpected. The situations, moreover, relate to three goals subsumed by liberal education: Knowledge—knowing that or what; Skills—knowing how; and Understanding—knowing why or wherefore. (Adler, 1983) As a proposal for revamping K-12 schooling, the Paideia proposal claims to address three essential goals: 1) Earning a living; 2) Being a good citizen; and 3) Living a full life. (Adler, 1984) The extent to which the Paideia proposal, or variations thereof, is incorporated into K-12 schooling remains to be seen. Its value as a model for the preparation for and initiation into liberal education should not be lost by adult educators.

Commentary

Unlike the curriculum models designed to achieve or enhance organizational effectiveness, the Paideia proposal is designed to make a broader impact. Its proponents claim the proposal will prepare students to earn a living, be a good citizen, and live a full life. Specific training for jobs is absolutely precluded, but an introduction to job and career opportunities is advised.

The Paideia group, consisting of scholars, authors, and educational leaders, has addressed the curriculum question of what constitutes the "good life" and responded by claiming a liberal education is the best assurance a good life will be realized. Given the goal of a liberal education, which is never fully attained and for which young people can only prepare, the Paideia proposal charts the means for working toward it.

Compared with organizational effectiveness, the goals for a liberal education are vague and varied. They actually are not goals as much as they are a process, i.e., becoming liberally educated, but never really achieving a liberal education. Evaluation is likewise going to be less definite and precise than in the models for organizational effectiveness.

The Paideia proposal is the preparation and introduction to a liberal education. It features three methods of teaching that revolve around three different purposes: didactic instruction to impart knowledge; coaching to introduce and improve basic skills; and Socratic questioning (in a seminar setting) to improve understanding. Content for the three methods varies as well: didactic instruction uses textbooks and teacher-made materials; coaching requires the students to demonstrate and practice basic skills (in effect, producing their own content); and seminar discussions involve not textbooks, but great works of imagination and exposition, a suggested list is provided in Adler, 1984.

The didactic teaching component that includes listening or reading presupposes an interest in listening or reading that may be less prevalent than the developers assume. As indicated earlier, teaching as telling has to be one of the least effective methodologies known. It may be indispensable to the Paideia model, but to the extent that it is, the entire model is weakened.

If one were interested in promoting a liberal education, the Paideia proposal outlines the preparation for attaining it. Indeed, its proponents argue a liberal education is basic. An extension of that argument is made in the promotion of the Great Books reading program and, in effect, the Great Books program can be viewed as the natural extension of seminar sessions of the Paideia proposal.

Great Books Discussion Groups

The *Great Books of the Western World* include 443 works by 74 authors. They span 2500 years of Western history, although more than one half of the selections were written between 1500 and 1900. The *Great Books of the Western World* embody what Hutchins (1952) calls the Great Conversation.

The selection of books was made by an advisory board consisting of scientists, novelists and academicians, all of whom had "devoted a large part of their lives to the education of adults" (Hutchins, 1952, p. xvi). Hutchins (1952) describes the origin of the selection procedure:

[Members of the Advisory Board] all sought to use great books for the purpose of educating adults. They determined to try to offer the means of liberal education in a coherent program. This set of books was the result (p. xvi).

The Advisory Board maintains:

. . . each book contributed in an important way to the Great Conversation. They do not claim that all the great books of the West are here . . . They would be disturbed (however) if they thought they had omitted books essential to a liberal education or had included any that had little bearing upon it (Hutchins, 1952, p. xvi).

The selections appear in chronological order and are classified, roughly, in color-coded volumes. The four categories of subject matter include:

- Epic and dramatic poetry, satires, and novels;

- Histories and works in ethics, economics, politics and jurisprudence;
- Mathematics and natural sciences—works in astronomy, physics, chemistry, biology, and psychology; and
- Philosophy and theology.

The Bible was omitted "only because Bibles are already widely distributed, and it was felt unnecessary to bring another, by way of this set, into homes that had several already" (Hutchins, 1952, p. xvii). References to the Bible, both the King James and the Douai versions, are made in the suggested reading lists.

The commitment to universal liberal education and the association of liberal education with the reading and discussion of the *Great Books* is clear:

> . . . the idea that liberal education is the education that everybody ought to have and the best way to a liberal education in the West is through the greatest works the West has produced, is still, in our view, the best educational idea there is (Hutchins, 1952, p. xiv).

One means by which adults can begin to achieve a liberal education is participation in a Great Books discussion group.

The Great Books Foundation, established in 1947 as a nonprofit educational corporation, "provides people of all ages with a lifelong program of liberal education through the reading and discussion of great works of literature" (Great Books Foundation (GBF), 1985, p. 13). The Foundation publishes, in paperback only, readings to be used in Great Books discussion groups. It also provides two-day training sessions for anyone interested in leading such groups. The Foundation publishes a Guide for Co-Leaders (all adult discussion groups are required to have two co-leaders) and a Guide for Participants. There is a Junior Great Books series, with graded readings from second grade through high school, but guidelines for the adult series will be discussed below.

Much like the seminar series of the Paideia Proposal discussed above, a Great Books discussion group is intended to increase understanding of the work being discussed as well as promote participants' self-reflection regarding their perceptions and values. Co-leaders are required to:

1. Ask questions that initiate, sustain, and conclude discussions of problems in the selection.

2. Ask questions that challenge unclear, factually incorrect, or contradictory statements.

3. Evaluate all responses according to their best judgment (GBF, 1985, p. 3).

In addition, "co-leaders should focus on statements that they want to question immediately; ignore uninteresting, trivial, or irrelevant statements; and table other statements for discussion later" (p. 3).

The Foundation (1985) lists and briefly discusses seventeen rules for co-leaders; the essential points of selected ones include:

1. Understand that you can ask three kinds of questions: fact, interpretation, and evaluation.
   a) Questions of fact require citing quotations or paraphrasing the material.
   b) Questions of interpretation require participants to explore the author's meaning.
   c) "Questions of evaluation ask participants to determine in what respects they agree or disagree with the author and to what extent the selection elucidates their lives" (p. 3).

2. "Stress questions of interpretation, but know when to ask questions of fact and evaluation" (p. 3). Interpretative questions can lead to an extended discussion of main ideas. They increase your knowledge because they are not easily answered—they challenge you to think. Basic interpretative questions are likely to generate opposing responses that will clarify and develop important ideas.

3. Use follow-up questions to probe the responses of participants and help the group to resolve the basic question.

4. Develop a discussion in depth by not settling for superficial answers. Use answers as the basis for new questions that will help the group to reach a deeper understanding of the material. Bear in mind, however, that some questions cannot be answered to everyone's satisfaction.

5. Do not use specialized or technical terms that are not included in the original material.

6. Listen carefully and include every participant.

7. Establish and maintain the following basic rules:
   a) The group may discuss only the selection assigned for the meeting or selections discussed at previous meetings.
   b) No participant who has not read the selection may take part in the discussion.

    c) Participants may not cite critics, historians, or other authorities.

    d) As a co-leader you may only ask questions. You may not introduce your opinions or comments.

    e) There must be two co-leaders for each discussion.

8. Discuss the selection in advance with your co-leader. Discuss and develop basic questions to be used with the group.

9. "Meet with your co-leader after the discussion. Answer two questions:

    a) Have we learned anything new as a result of our discussion?

    b) What could we have done to improve the discussion" (p. 8).

The discussion can last from one to two hours, depending on how actively the members are participating. At the end of the session the members should decide on the next selection to be read for the next group discussion.

Commentary

The Great Books discussion groups rely on volunteer participants. Subject matter is drawn from the *Great Books of the Western World* exclusively. The commitment of proponents of the groups is three-fold:

1. A liberal education is the best basic education;
2. Every adult should begin/continue a liberal education (one never finishes); and
3. Reading and discussing the Great Books is the best way to become liberally educated.

This liberal education curriculum model is closed in that content for it is essentially predetermined and the only method for studying is reading and discussion.

Unlike the Paideia proposal, which is promoted as preparation for liberal education and uses three different teaching-learning modes, the Great Books discussion group makes exclusive use of the seminar mode. Prerequisites of some minimal knowledge base and, more important, basic skills such as reading and speaking, are assumed before conducting the discussion sessions.

The special needs of learners are disregarded if responding to them would interfere with content selection or group discussion of content.

Proponents of the discussion group make no claim for it being able to accommodate all adults. It is no surprise that the Paideia proposal, designed as a preparation for liberal education is promoted by the same leaders who initiated the Great Books discussion groups thirty years earlier.

The Bachelor of Liberal Studies and Let's Talk About It Program

S till within the purpose of liberal education, the Bachelor of Liberal Studies and Let's Talk About It programs can be viewed as variations of the models used by the Paideia proposal and Great Books discussion groups respectively. The major difference between the models described below and the two described in the previous chapter is the opening up of content selection to include a wider variety of subject matter.

The Bachelor of Liberal Studies

The Bachelor of Liberal Studies (BLS) is a nontraditional, institution-affiliated, undergraduate degree program. It was established in 1961 and is administered by the College of Liberal Studies of the University of Oklahoma.

BLS students engage in a combination of independent studies and short-term seminars. The three areas of humanities, natural sciences, and social sciences are represented in both the independent study mode and the seminar format. A fourth area, called inter-area, integrates the previous three areas of study. Within the BLS program the humanities include philosophy, cultural history, literature, and the fine arts. The natural sciences include the biological sciences of biochemistry, microbiology, botany, and zoology; the earth sciences of geology, oceanography, physical geography, and astronomy; and the physical sciences of physics, mathematics, and chemistry. The social sciences include anthropology, economics, history, geography, political science, psychology, and sociology.

The BLS program is essentially self-paced, and the area seminars are held twice a year, which means a student would never have to wait more than six months to complete an area. Figure 4.1 depicts the entire BLS program. The independent study mode and the area seminars will be described below.

Area independent study mode. After admission and placement testing to detect academic skill deficiencies, if any, the student selects an area of study to begin his or her program. The independent study

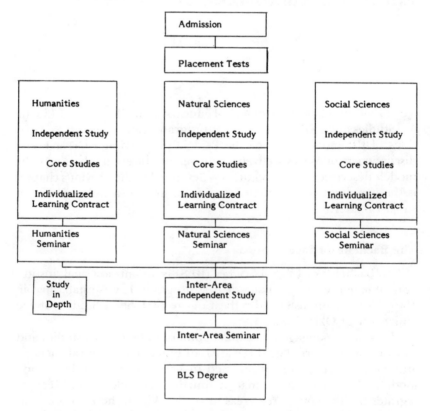

Figure 4.1   *The Bachelor of Liberal Studies Program (College of Liberal Studies Bulletin, 1985–86, p. 9).*

mode has two parts: a core area, consisting of twelve to fifteen books that are assigned as part of the guided independent study and a learning contract that is designed by the student and faculty advisor cooperatively. The learning contract includes study experiences that meet specific needs or goals established by the student.

> Contracts may address career development interests or areas of personal interest . . . (the) contract should be geared toward an understanding of the interrelationship of specialized knowledge and the broader field of the student's area study (College of Liberal Studies Bulletin, 1985–86, p. 8).

Several strategies may be used to satisfy the learning contract, including a reading program, enrollment in conventional course work, or special work assignments that capitalize on unique employment opportunities combined with readings or other experiences.

After the twelve to fifteen books of the core reading assignment are read and studied and the learning contract is completed, the student, with the permission of the advisor, takes a comprehensive examination. The examination includes essay and objective questions. Assessment for the test can be "pass," "pass with deficiency" and "restudy-retest." If the assessment is "pass with deficiency," additional reading assignments will be made by the advisor. If the results are "restudy-retest" a substantial amount of additional reading will be required as well as later taking another form of the examination. Students complete their independent study in three areas—humanities, natural sciences, and social sciences, plus a final inter-area.

Area seminars. After successfully completing the area's independent study and passing the comprehensive examination, the student may enroll in the area seminar. Each seminar is team taught by at least two faculty members from the main campus. Seminars are scheduled for a ten day period in December/January and a similar time period in the summer.

Each seminar is designed to explore in depth a major problem or theme. Topics for the seminar are determined by the faculty team; lectures, demonstrations, discussions, field trips and other activites are designed around the theme. The Bulletin (1985–86) indicates the multiple objectives for each seminar:

1. Consider ideas and knowledge gained through independent study and any prior college course work.
2. Acquire, organize and synthesize new knowledge, data and ideas

relating to the theme of the seminar and to prepare analyses of problems.

3. Test personal knowledge and convictions through discussion with members of the faculty teaching team and with other seminar students.
4. Improve personal skill in oral and written presentation of ideas.
5. Develop objectivity in problem analysis through examination of differing viewpoints (p.8).

Examples of seminar themes are; "Energy: Implications for Change," "The Modernist Revolution: New Forms and Meanings in the Arts and Literature, 1890–1960," and "Symbolic Structure and Human Values" (Bulletin, 1985–86, p. 9).

Inter-area independent study mode. After completing the three area independent studies and the three area seminars following each, students begin an inter-area independent study. This interdisciplinary study involves the reading and critiquing of several core books that have interdisciplinary themes. In addition, the student selects other similar books from a list approved by the college faculty and reads and critiques them as well.

Another phase of the inter-area independent study is the study in depth. The student proposes a study that may be a research paper on a specific subject or a creative work in literature, science, or the arts. A faculty advisor from a relevant area is assigned to supervise successful completion of the study in depth.

Inter-area seminar. This final seminar focuses on an interdisciplinary theme and is team taught by faculty from the humanities, natural sciences, and social sciences. The inter-area seminars are three weeks in length and offered twice a year. Examples of themes from the inter-area seminars include: "Freedom and Authority," "The Limits of Knowledge: Facts, Theories, and Models," and "Arcadia—Reality or Myth."

Commentary

The BLS program is designed for adults who want a liberal education bachelor's degree. The subject matter may include selections from but is not limited to the *Great Books of the Western World*. In comparison with the Paideia proposal, the BLS is very similar except that didactic instruction is almost exclusively through reading and independent study. The coaching of the Paideia proposal, wherein basic skills are developed and practiced, does not occur within the BLS program, except for relatively advanced levels of skill development. Finally, the two seminars are quite similar in that they emphasize thematic concerns and promote deeper understanding of the independent study materials.

The BLS program requires more independent study (reading and critiquing) than most programs. The generalist approach, which is what a liberal education is, is consistently promoted through interdisciplinary readings and thematic seminars that are team taught. Although a majority of the readings are required, students can select readings based on their interests and the study in depth is entirely of the student's choosing.

Let's Talk About It

Discussion groups have been formed for as long as adults have been reading books of mutual interest. The Great Books discussion group, described in the previous chapter, probably has attracted the largest number of participants since its inception in the 1950s. A new discussion group has emerged, however, that is gaining rapidly in popularity.

Funded by the National Endowment for the Humanities and sponsored by the Association of Specialized and Cooperative Library Agencies, a division of the American Library Association, the "Let's Talk About It" program has as a general goal "to promote the development of reading and discussion programs in America's public libraries" (Moores & Rubin, 1984, p. v). More specifically, the program seeks:

> . . . to promote the creation of humanities reading and discussion series in libraries nationwide while also adding to the traditional participant/librarian/discussion leader partnership a vital member: the humanities scholar (Moores & Rubin, 1984, p. 3).

The reason for including the scholar from the humanities is to capitalize on the scholar's expertise regarding the book, author, or topic being discussed by the group.

The potential subject matter, i.e., books from the humanities, for the "Let's Talk About It" series includes selections from "the studies of language, history, philosophy, literature, jurisprudence, archaeology, anthropology, ethics, comparative religion, the history and appreciation of the arts, and certain social sciences" (Moores & Rubin, 1984, p. 3). Moores & Rubin (1984) maintain that as disparate as these fields might seem, a common element joins them: the search to understand the infinite mysteries of human existence. What are the links of the past to the present? What is the moral basis for the decisions we must make each day? How do we find full self-expression while at the same time coexisting with one another in peace (p. 3)?

One assumption is that the literature from the humanities helps readers give meaning to the human experience. And another assumption is that the humanities take on more meaning as the participants relate their ideas and life experiences to the literature. The scholar's role is to add the expert's perspective to the potential meanings residing within the participants. (Moores & Rubin, 1984) All of the potential for meaning is better realized through discussion.

The program. The format for the program, to which variations could be made, is a ten-week series on a theme, such as "Work," "The Quest for the American Dream," or any other that a planning committee decides. Five books related to the theme are designated by a planning committee that includes a humanities scholar, and every two weeks the group meets to discuss one of the books. The meeting length is about two hours, with the scholar speaking for thirty to forty minutes, small group discussion led by volunteers taking forty to fifty minutes, and a reconvening of the total group for additional discussion, questions, or summaries taking another fifteen to thirty minutes.

The initial presentation by the scholar could address the author's background, the relevance of the book to the series' theme, main points made within the book, and any other relevant points. The intent of having the scholar is to have him or her bring a richness and broader perspective to the reading. (Moores & Rubin, 1984)

All who participate in the series, or even attend just one meeting, are likely to benefit:

> . . . participants and discussion leaders because they gain new insights into the books they have just read, scholars because they are reaching and learning from new audiences with deep and varied life experiences, and librarians because they attract new users, serve longtime users in additional ways, and further establish the library as a vital community resource (Moores & Rubin, 1984, p. 5).

Perhaps the point about increasing library use—from new as well as established users—is the strongest link with the goals of liberal education because it reinforces the idea that lifelong learning is what a liberal education entails.

The planning committee. A representative committee of five to eight members is recommended. (Moores & Rubin, 1984) They should include the program director, one or more community members (trustee, Friend of the Library, or interested patron) one of whom could be a resource for raising funds to sponsor the program, at least one scholar from the humanities who can help to select themes, designate appropriate books and perhaps make one of the presentations in the series, and one person who is willing to help to promote the series within the community. The overall responsibilities of the planning committee include:

1. To discuss—and revise, if necessary—goals and objectives that the program director has outlined.
2. To define the audience in the community that would be most interested in attending the series.
3. To help reach that target audience.
4. To determine the theme topic to be used in the series.
5. To suggest organizations or individuals who have a special knowledge of the theme subject area and would be helpful in selecting related materials.
6. To help select scholars to make program presentations.
7. To suggest individuals in the community who have had training or experience in leading group discussion (Moores & Rubin, 1984, p. 11).

Theme development. As indicated above the series has selected themes, but each program, through its planning committee, could create its own. Whether selected or created, several criteria need to be applied to determine appropriateness for the local site:

1. Will the theme have relevance to people in your community, particularly your target audience, the out-of-school adult (or segments of this population)?
2. Will the theme provoke constructive controversy and discussion?
3. Will the theme appeal to both men and women?
4. Will the theme allow for a diversity of opinion and a range of books and authors?
5. Will the theme encourage series participants to use other materials and services that the library offers, such as reference, films, videotapes, audiovisual equipment, etc. (Moores & Rubin, 1984, p. 12)?

Exact answers will not be possible to all the questions of criteria, but consensus of committee members should be sought with regard to each of them. Using experience to guide subsequent series will be helpful.

Book selection and distribution. As with the issue of selecting or creating a theme for the series, a number of criteria are suggested for book selection. (Moores & Rubin, 1984).

1. Will the book (for each meeting) stimulate serious discussion?
2. What is the book's appeal? Informational, humorous, inspirational? If possible, a balance should be achieved over the ten-week session. Length of book and genre should be considered the same way, i.e., seek a balance, overall.
3. Is the book available in paperback? Cost to the library or participant makes this question critical.
4. Are other related materials available in the library for follow-up interests, if these occur?

The committee's best guess may have to serve with regard to answering all of these questions until experience is gained in the program.

Moores and Rubin (1984) discuss other program considerations, e.g., variations of format, potential audiences, scheduling, budget, and evaluation. The essential features of purpose, format, the planning committee, and selecting themes and content are sufficiently described above to permit inferences about the curriculum aspects of this program.

Commentary

The "Let's Talk About It" reading and discussion series is designed to promote reading in the humanities and enhance the understanding of same through scholarly perspective and small group discussion. Content is selected by others, not the participants. Prerequisite skills of reading and the ability to articulate ideas and opinions are assumed. As was the case in the Great Books discussion group, no provision is made for developing skills that are at too low a level to participate effectively.

The series is associated with the American Library Association and seeks, among other goals, to enhance the service and status of public libraries. By using a thematic approach, the series is consistent with its liberal education goal of promoting a generalist as opposed to specialist approach. Use of a humanities scholar adds a dimension of richness to the discussion but creates the risk of participants being intimidated from offering their own impressions and interpretations of the readings. Unlike the Great Book discussion groups, reading material may be of the twentieth century and expert opinion is included, by way of the scholar.

All four of the liberal education models presuppose an interest that serves as sufficient motivation to participate in any of the programs. The voluntary aspect of adult education may be nowhere more evident than in programs designed to promote liberal education.

SECTION III

ADULT BASIC EDUCATION

The proponents of universal liberal education, specifically, Hutchins and Adler, as was seen in the previous section, argue forcefully that a liberal education ought to be considered basic for everyone. But basic education, as it will be described in this section, is rudimentary skill development. The vast majority of programs referred to as Adult Basic Education (ABE) are aimed at improving fundamental skills of reading and other language arts.

The Paideia proposal, described in Chapter 3, includes a skill development emphasis. The primary source of content within this emphasis was the student's own productions/creations and the primary teaching method was coaching. Drill, practice, and homework were all required to establish and refine the basic intellectual skills that would be used in subsequent learning. The extent to which coaching, or some variation thereof, is appropriate within literacy programs remains to be seen.

Although adult basic education includes high school equivalency programs that prepare individuals for the general educational development (GED) test and English as a second language, neither will be included in this section for two reasons: First, space does not permit treating them here. Second, the GED programs typically are sponsored and funded by states and other agencies with different funding sources in cooperation with local school districts, all of which makes generalizations about them very difficult (Smith, 1984). Models for teaching English as a second language will not be included because the number of ESL students who are illiterate constitute less than one-fifth of the semi-literate and illiterate adults for whom literacy programs are planned (Kozol, 1985).

Before examining suggested models and methods of adult basic education, it is important to establish the magnitude of the problem facing adult educators, i.e., how many Americans need ABE? Figures from various U.S. offices and agencies are not all alike, nor do they agree with independent estimates. Kozol (1985), after reviewing several conflicting estimates and conferring with the directors of comprehensive attempts of estimation, concludes that sixty million adults, over one third of the 1984 adult population, should be called "illiterate in terms of U.S. print communication at the present time" (p. 10).

The federal government began addressing the adult basic education problem in a more intensive manner in the 1960s, with the passage of legislation aimed at enhancing education and stemming poverty in the United States. ABE became Title III of the Elementary and Secondary Education Act, known as the Adult Education Act of 1966 and later ABE became Title VI of the Educational Amendments of 1974. This relatively short history of intense federal support has nonetheless yielded professional response to the problem in terms of books or models or strategies associated with ABE.

Chapter 5 will describe one general model for literacy education and Chapter 6 will examine the model of literacy education employed by Paulo Freire.

A Literacy Curriculum Model*

Newman (1980) presents a "highly flexible and generative model" (p. x) to guide ABE teachers in helping adults achieve basic literacy. Although Newman calls it an instructional model, it will be considered here as a curriculum model because it outlines what is involved in providing access to knowledge and skills. Figure 5.1 illustrates the various parts of the model and their interrelationships. Each component will be briefly discussed below. For more specific discussion, it is recommended that the original source (Newman, 1980) be consulted.

Overview.

The first phase of the model represents an overall orientation that is needed to guide subsequent decisions that will be made as one works through the model in assisting adults to read. Newman states, "In order to plan and implement successful instruction, the teacher or tutor should make every effort to discover who the students really are" (p. 3). The impulse to stereotype the adult who seeks literacy training should be resisted. Newman discusses four influences that

---

*For a more detailed account of the model, see Newman's *Adult Basic Education: Reading* (1980). Unless otherwise indicated, all references in this chapter will be from this source.

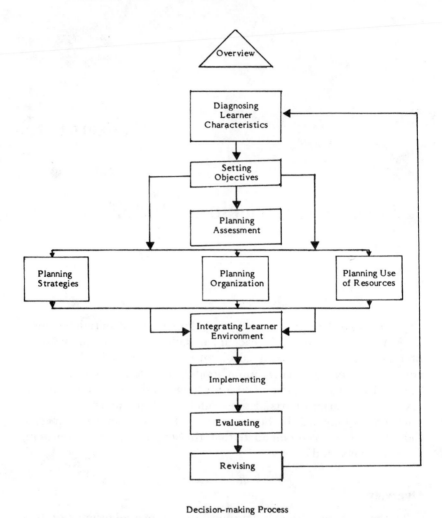

Decision-making Process

Figure 5.1   *A Literacy Curriculum Model (Newman, A.P. and Harste, J.C., "RELATE*
Instructional Process" [Bloomington: Indiana Univ., 1976] in Newman,
1980, p. 46).

affect all adults and demonstrates how knowledge of the four can help
in planning and providing literacy training.

Cultural influences, including dialect, values, and living patterns
should be discovered and used to advantage whenever possible. Inquiry must be discreet into areas that can be sensitively guarded for
fear of humiliation. Some cultural influences may have a negative

bearing on learning to read. Nonstandard English, for example, can be a handicap for beginning adult readers, but until they recognize a need to change the usage, it should be accepted and welcomed into the learning process.

Newman claims "students are particularly appreciative of the teacher who is genuinely interested in family activities and values, educational and work experiences, and makes imaginative use of these in the instructional process" (p. 5). In addition to cultural background of the student, the teacher needs to be aware of other factors that can affect the student.

Physiological influences can take their toll on any learner and the ABE teacher should be knowledgeable of those affecting the adults seeking literacy training. Flexibility and a willingness to accommodate special needs are critical characteristics for the provider of literacy training to have. Adults, for example, may come to a learning session after spending long hours working and experiencing a great deal of stress. The appropriate response of the provider would be offering frequent breaks and being relaxed in manner. Vision and hearing problems should be compensated for by providing ample lighting or special seating arrangements. Small muscle control needed for handling a pen or pencil may be lacking in adults who have not been writing for years and have not developed these abilities.

Two other effects of physiological influence mentioned by Newman are absenteeism and "school" induced headaches. Chronic illness or unstable family setting could contribute to excessive absences. Telephone calls or other inquiries reflecting the teacher's concern for the student might encourage the student to attend more regularly. Unpleasant memories of previous schooling experiences could have physiological implications. Newman cites the case of an adult student who suffered severe headaches when attending ABE classes, only to have them disappear after successfuly completing the classes.

Psychological influences that appear to have a significant impact on ABE students are fear, lack of hope, and indifference. Newman suggests frequent indications of success are important to ABE students who fear failure. Scaling lessons down to manageable size, perhaps one page stories instead of six page stories, will permit the student to realize some measure of success in every lesson. Teacher attitude is critical to success of ABE students. Newman summarizes this aspect:

> Generally educators who work with ABE students want to appreciate the sensibilities of others. It is important, therefore, that they be alert to their own reactions that might indicate prejudice, superiority, or condescension.

Educators need to make a special effort to understand the habits, cultures, and beliefs of those who often live lives very different from theirs (p. 7).

The indifference many nonreading adults feel toward ABE programs probably is the biggest deterrent to participation. Whether indifference is caused by poor schooling experiences of the past or a sense of hopelessness for the future, the ABE teacher should be aware that those students who do show up may still be suffering negative attitudes about the prospects for change. Newman advises, "the challenge of changing these attitudes is formidable, but not final, given patience and large doses of imagination" (p. 8).

Finally, educational influences, such as poor diagnosis of reading ability in the early years or simply poor previous teaching, can have adverse effects on the adult nonreader. Rather than accepting another person's diagnosis of reading ability, Newman advises personal assessment to detect difficulties that may impede reading progress. Her antidote for poor schooling experiences of the past includes providing large amounts of praise for work well done, minimizing mistakes, and sharing the joy of learning.

In addition to being aware of the above four influences on adult nonreaders, Newman suggests preparing a definition of reading that will aid in setting goals and objectives later in the process. The definition should include theoretical concerns, social needs, and instructional requirements.

At the theoretical level, a working definition of reading should include consideration for the following;

1. What happens when a person reads?
2. What is the purpose of reading?
3. How does reading fit with such aspects of communication as listening, speaking, and writing?
4. Should writing and reading be combined?
5. Does a person's background influence his reading ability? Why? How?
6. Does this theoretical portion of your statement apply equally to children and adults (pp. 10–11)?

After drafting such a statement, Newman recommends discussing it with others and revising as necessary.

In similar fashion, Newman suggests considering social needs in the definition of reading. Different occupations and life roles create different demands for literacy.

Being a "good citizen" by voting and taking an active role in civic or neighborhood affairs, for example, will require certain reading abilities beyond those of a specialized occupation.

Instructional aspects of a reading definition include determining goals and objectives to be achieved by the student. Broad goals typically contain specific objectives that can be used for specific lessons. The broad goals are useful for overall planning and function as general guides for planning a program. Examples of instructional goals include:

1. The learner, with material at the appropriate reading level, will comprehend what is read.
2. The learner will read information when faced with a problem.
3. The learner will read for enjoyment.
4. The learner will read and interpret directions accurately.
5. The learner will choose to read regularly (p. 12).

All of the effort to articulate a definition of reading that includes the theoretical, social, and instructional considerations will help the ABE teacher remain sensitive to purpose and goals when beginning to plan a literacy program for a nonreading adult. A prerequisite, in addition to the above, is a diagnosis of learner characteristics, which will be described below.

Diagnosing learner characteristics.

The name of the general system by which ABE, as well as most other reading teachers, teach reading is the diagnostic-prescriptive. The first phase, once one is oriented and sensitized to the myriad influences on the nonreader, is diagnosis. Newman discusses three means by which the ABE teacher can diagnose learner characteristics: an informal interest inventory, an informal reading inventory, and standardized tests.

An informal interest inventory (III) is a record of background information that could help a teacher diagnose reading difficulties, identify interests and attitudes, including negative ones, and be an aid in choosing resources and strategies to use with the learner. The III is intended to be a friendly inquiry into family, use of leisure time, past school experiences, and other areas that reveal learner characteristics. Although the III will not reveal specific difficulties with reading, it should enable the teacher to tailor methods and resources more personally. Knowledge of family relationships, favorite TV shows, hobbies, etc., provides possibilities for reading exercises in areas of interest to the student. In addition, to the extent that the III reveals motives for attending an ABE class, the teacher can appeal to these to encourage perseverance in the class.

An informal reading inventory (IRI) should yield more specific information on actual reading difficulties, but Newman recommends using an interest inventory first, followed by a reading inventory. By having students read passages that are of varying difficulty, the teacher has an opportunity to make note of specific problems. In addition to estimating reading ability level from hearing the student read aloud from graded material, notes can be taken with regard to the kinds of errors a student makes. Unfamiliar words might be replaced by familiar ones, or simply omitted. Reversals of letters, prolonged hesitation, and other difficulties should be marked on the teacher's copy of the material being read. This information will be useful in later assignments. Comprehension questions can be asked to check on the degree to which the reader understood the material.

An IRI can be used for the nonreading adult by assembling a series of pictures and having the student make up captions for each and subsequently reading the captions. An IRI also could include assessment of recognizing letters of the alphabet and recognition of words from basic sight word lists.

Standardized tests can be useful in diagnosing reading difficulties, Newman suggests, as long as the following conditions can be met:

1. the standardized instructions for administering the test are followed;
2. the population on which the test has been based includes the age, ethnic, and racial characteristics of the learners being tested;
3. the entire test will be used if reporting is necessary and not just portions of it; and
4. taking the test will not intimidate or unduly discourage the learners.

Newman discusses the advantages for using standardized tests, e.g., access to national norms, ease in administration, and reliability of results, but reminds the ABE teachers that the validity of the tests depends on whether or not they measure what has been or will be taught.

Regardless of what specific teacher-made or standardized instruments are used for diagnosis, the intent is to gather information about the learner that will be useful in reducing resistance to learning and providing insights for the selection of appropriate goals and objectives for reading achievement. Establishing goals and objectives is the next step in the diagnostic-prescriptive teaching process.

Setting objectives.

Diagnosis leads to establishing goals and objectives. Distinguishing between goals, which are typically broad and general, and objectives, which are typically narrow and specific, is important to planning for instruction and checking on progress. An example of the relationship between goals and objectives is illustrated in the following sample of goals and supporting objectives.

1. The learner will enjoy reading.
   a. The learner will read a comic strip for entertainment.
   b. The learner will read a magazine for entertainment.
   c. The learner will read a book for entertainment.
2. The learner will read to solve life problems.
   a. The learner will be able to read a machine repair manual.
   b. The learner will be able to read in order to file a report.
3. The learner will read for information.
   a. The learner will be able to get information from a book.
   b. The learner will be able to get information from a newspaper.
   c. The learner will be able to get information from a magazine.
4. The learner will read critically.
   a. The learner will be able to discriminate between fact and fiction.
   b. The learner will be able to recognize an author's bias (pp. 34–5).

Newman notes that traditionally goals and objectives have been classified according to , "knowing" or "cognitive," "feelings" or "affective," and "physical" or "psychomotor," and such classification can be helpful when planning specific instructional strategies. Whether the three-domain classification is used, or some other, the important concern is that the goals and objectives grow out of the expressed needs and interests of the learner.

Published professional sources of goals and objectives are available from the work of the Adult Performance Level Project (Lyman, 1977, pp. 188–192), the National Assessment of Educational Progress (Lyman, 1977, pp. 182–188), and the *Seventy-Sixth Yearbook* of the National Society for the Study of Education (Squire, 1977, pp. 88–89). Newman notes the caution that should be exercised in using goals and objectives developed by others. She considers it imperative that goals and objectives reflect a student's interests, needs, and abilities. When possible, teacher and student should develop the goals together. The effort should be a blend of what the student feels is appropriate and what the teacher believes is necessary for the student to experience success. Attaining objectives and goals is an indicator of success and devising means by which these indicators can be experienced is the next step in the model.

Planning assessment.

When assessment is planned it often becomes more apparent why specific objectives are so convenient. If an objective is "to find names in a telephone directory," then securing a telephone directory and having the student look up names is about all that is needed to assess whether or not the objective has been achieved. Time may be a factor in such an objective, but even using some length of time as a criterion, the assessment of the objective is relatively straightforward.

When objectives contain vague words open to several differing interpretations, assessment becomes something of a challenge and more of a gamble. A challenge because the instructor must specify some kind of observable performance, the successful completion of which will permit inferring the objective has been attained. The gamble is that whatever behaviors or performances are identified for assessment do indeed reflect the original objective. "Managing one's own finances," for example, is a worthy objective, but it certainly is open to a number of interpretations.

Newman further cautions that not all learners have the same needs with regard to objectives, i.e., an objective is only appropriate if it reflects actual needs and interests of the learner. And even if two learners shared the same objective, the time required for one to attain it could be different from the other. The point is that not all students will have the same objectives and that, if and when they do, their rates of progress toward it are likely to be different.

Typically, when instruction is geared to an individual's goals and objectives, the assessment is a criterion-referenced type. The learner either successfully passes, according to preestablished criteria (level of difficulty, time, etc.) or does not pass. The other type of assessment is norm-referenced, which relates how the learner performed in comparison with others who took the same test. Norm-referenced tests frequently yield percentile scores that indicate the percentage of the group, on whom the test was based, who made lower scores. For the poor test taker who has not progressed far in reading achievement, the probability is great that the percentile score will be very low or not even high enough to register. Newman advises not using a test if the likelihood is that the student will be discouraged by the results.

The use of any test must be kept in perspective. It may be, for example, that a test contains items that are not part of the goals and objectives for a particular learner. The teacher should realize that the only legitimate assessment is over that which has been consciously pursued. And if tests are used ahead of time to determine goals and objectives, it can become a case of the tail wagging the dog. Determining the appropriateness of a test is the instructor's responsibility. Makers of standardized tests usually report estimates of the test's validity and reliability, as well as describe the group on whom the test was based.

The validity of a test is the assurance that the test indeed measures what it says it measures. Reliability is an estimate of how consistent the scores would be if the test were retaken an infinite number of times. Reliability estimates can range from .00 to 1.00, with coefficients in the .80s and .90s considered good. The group on whom the test was standardized should have characteristics similar to those of the adults being tested, i.e., age, race, educational backgrounds should at least be comparable.

Finally, assessment planning includes maintaining student records. Newman illustrates a number of examples, but suffice it here to indicate that checklists can be appropriate, as well as actual examples of oral reading (recorded on tapes), and a list of stories read or written that reflects progress toward goals.

Planning strategies.

Once the goals and objectives are developed, with an eye toward assessment, as was just described, the instructor next considers teaching/learning strategies that will enable the student to work toward attainment. Newman considers three critical variables involved in making strategy decisions. These are: the learner, the teacher, and the content. All three interact and affect the strategy decisions.

The most stable component in the trilogy of learner, teacher, and content is the content. Learners and teachers vary considerably in their styles of learning and teaching. And when learners are examined carefully regarding their learning needs, even the content can be different for different learners. Choosing strategy then, is a matter of looking "for methods that are both compatible with style of teaching and uniquely satisfying to the learner" (p. 65). Four approaches to teaching reading are discussed by Newman. Each will be described briefly below.

The Language Experience Approach uses the student's base of listening, speaking, reading, and writing experiences to develop skills in same. Stories or experiences are dictated to the instructor who transcribes them to make them available as reading material to be read by the student who produced them. Students may help one another in making stories into "material," for example, a newsletter might be created that uses contributions from all students. The essential point is that the written material comes from the student, rather than from some other source and being imposed on the student.

Patterns in Language is an area Newman believes is often overlooked by reading teachers. Patterns in sentences—placement of subject verb, and object—are well developed as oral language skills in many adult nonreaders. The patterns approach is intended to capitalize on the student's knowledge of oral patterns in learning to read.

Word Analysis skills include context, picture clues, phonics, sight vocabulary, and structural analysis. How each skill is used with a student will depend on that student's needs and interests.

Structural Analysis focuses on compound words and special prefixes and suffixes. Learning about the structure of some words can aid in spelling as well as help in expanding vocabulary.

Newman discusses four aspects of learning theory and how they can be applied to ABE teaching. The aspects include incentive, practice, reinforcement, and transfer.

Incentive concerns a student's desire or motivation to seek assistance. That motivation can be hidden and fragile. The instructor needs to be sensitive to the various reasons adults participate and not inadvertently take away the student's motivation. A general rule Newman suggests is to consistently try to connect the learning to the student's needs.

Practice is necessary for skill development. Newman advises using the student's own material from language experience stories as content from which practice exercises can be developed. Practice can include language patterns, word analysis skills, and understanding prefixes and suffixes. The use of the student's material will help reduce, but not preclude, the boredom associated with practice.

Reinforcement, like practice, is made easier when the material used is derived from the student. The use of context, for example, will reinforce meanings of words and familiar context is easier to work with than unfamiliar context. Newman claims there is a built-in reinforcement whenever material produced by the student is used for furthering the understanding of the reading process.

Transfer means applying what is learned in one setting to another. Transfer is enhanced if the first setting has elements similar to those in the second. Some classrooms, for example, are so sterile and unlike other parts of the community that transfer is impeded. The instructor needs to include elements or procedures that are like the real-life settings where application of literacy skills will be expected.

The choice of a specific reading approach—language experience, language patterns, word analysis, or structural analysis—will depend on the teacher's preference and the student's needs. The approaches are not mutually exclusive—each has been treated separately for the convenience of description. The four learning theory principles can be used with any or all of the reading approaches. Newman underscores the necessity, however, of meeting the needs of students, irrespective of whatever reading approach, or combination of approaches, is used. The four principles of learning theory are relatively easily applied when needs and interests of students are kept in mind by the instructor. Equipped with the ability to use different reading approaches and aware of how to apply learning principles throughout, the ABE instructor can choose from a wide array of general strategies, any of which can be appropriate for meeting the needs of students.

Newman discusses eleven general strategies for ABE teachers. Each has its advantages and disadvantages, depending on a number of factors, and the skillful teacher will pick and choose from among them once student needs and interests are known.

Planning organization.

Determining how time, place, and people will be organized requires a consideration of learner characteristics, content, and objectives. Newman offers some generalizations and guidelines regarding the when, where, and who questions. She notes, for example, that frequently time and place are dictated by administrative decisions. She recommends meeting at least twice a week for one or two hours. Schools are frequently the site for ABE classes, but other locations may be more comfortable and accessible. She encourages use of the public library, YMCA or YWCA or even a work place, if accommodations can be arranged. The disadvantages of using a school include scheduling at night, often inappropriate furniture and seating arrangements, and the fact that many, if not most, ABE students have had unpleasant past associations with schools, thus presenting another hurdle to overcome.

The organization of people can be guided by several considerations. Ideally, students should be grouped, according to Newman,

> . . . together with other students who, it is hoped, will gain the most from working with each other. Such groupings—whether small, large, or on a student-tutor basis—should vary according to the objectives being pursued (p. 95).

The challenge is to maintain interest in the instruction. Newman suggests individualizing lessons whenever possible and notes the development of cassette tapes that can be used for listening and reading at the same time. Possibly the instructor could make such tapes, but time and resources may be too limited for completely individualizing through such technical aids. Furthermore, Newman cautions, "tapes and mechanical devices can never replace the personal touch when working with ABE students, although they may supplement or reinforce" (p. 96). Newman summarizes the concern for organization by tying together the elements of time, place, and people. She claims, "when sufficient attention is given to the instruction-related aspects of time, to providing pleasant and workable areas for learning, and to seeing that individual needs are met, those students whose lives may have been in a fog of indifference and failure can be more readily encouraged to see the possibilities that lie ahead" (p. 96).

Planning resources.

Newman advises that the most important, most basic resource to the ABE instructor is the ABE student. When the instructor knows something of the student's background experiences, former jobs, and current interests, collected from the informal interest inventory or other interaction, the instructor can use reading materials that pertain to them. Such personal concern is likely to maintain student interest because the material is within the student's experience and will undoubtedly increase the chances for early success. Finding or developing reading material that is related to the adult student's interest is a challenge and Newman suggests several sources of free or inexpensive materials.

Community agencies can be helpful resources. Newman describes the Literacy Volunteers of America, Inc., founded in Syracuse in 1962. It has a network of local affiliates who recruit students, train volunteers, and develop reading materials for beginning readers.

Public libraries represent an important free resource to ABE programs. Not only do they have reading materials at all levels over many subjects, they may be able to provide rooms for meetings.

Bookstores may be able to provide free or low cost materials to an ABE program. Paperback books that do not sell well frequently are discarded, save the cover, which is returned to the publisher. The same is true for comic books. A bookstore manager might be willing to donate coverless books to an ABE program.

Some industries support ABE programs and may provide teaching/learning sites or contribute money to purchase other resources.

Schools have a long tradition in providing space, usually in the evening, and other resources for ABE programs. Schools should not be overlooked when considering community resources, especially volunteer instructors.

Churches, private schools, and agencies like the YWCA and YMCA may be good sources for space, volunteers, or reading materials. The chamber of commerce, for example, typically has brochures and pamphlets about the community that are free or inexpensive.

Newspapers, tape recorders, films, and television are other resources discussed by Newman. In addition, she describes commercial materials and criteria for choosing them. Included in this section is a discussion of the use of readability formulas and appropriate cautions regarding their shortcomings.

Integrating learning.

Newman recommends the use of unit teaching as a way to integrate the many interests and different abilities typically found in an ABE class. The unit approach is relevant for individual tutoring experiences as well, because it provides a theme around which many exercises can be constructed and a variety of student contributions can be appropriate.

The nature of the unit is limited only by the imagination of the instructor. Newman offers examples such as developing a cookbook or simply compiling various favorite recipes. A kind of consumer economics or other unifying theme about wise shopping and purchasing might be used as a common concern for a period of time. The length of unit, like its nature, will depend on the interests of the students. Some units may last a week or two, while others could be sustained, if student interest is sufficient, for six months or a year.

The specific reading strategies—language experience, language patterns, word analysis, and structural analysis—can be utilized within the unit. The important point is that the unit provides an overall meaning to what might otherwise become isolated and sterile exercises. Newman also addresses reading rate as a concern for new adult readers. She claims reading rate is not particularly meaningful for readers who are below a fourth grade reading level, but that they typically have an interest in it, nonetheless. She recommends the instructor make it clear that rate depends on the material being read and the specific purpose for which the reading is being done.

Implementation.

Newman provides a chronological account of an actual ABE student whom she and her colleagues tutored for thirty-one months. The chronicle reveals specific application of the recommendations made throughout the book. No attempt will be made to summarize the detailed account provided by Newman.

Evaluation of student/instructor progress.

Whereas assessement is performed to ascertain how a student is progressing with regard to a specific objective, evaluation encompasses a broader array of activities. The very assessment procedures used and subsequent decisions made are themselves activities that need to be evaluated.

Every instructional decision ought to be made after some kind of evaluation, but typically, formal evaluation occurs after a specified time or the end of a unit. If there is a sponsoring agency for the ABE program, it should be responsible for the evaluation. If a tutor or instructor is working without a sponsoring agency, then evaluation is the instructor's responsibility.

Evaluating student progress should include the following guidelines:

1. Evaluation must be made against the broad goals and specific objectives that were used.
2. Generally, data to be collected during or after completion of instruction should be specified in advance. This might include data needed by a principal or program chairman (e.g., when the results of standardized tests may be needed), or data you will need later when determining whether a goal or objective has been reached (Does the learner set purposes before reading?).
3. Informal evaluation should be on-going even though formal evaluation may have to be conducted at specific times (pp. 174– 75).

In addition to evaluating student progress, other elements of the curriculum should be considered.

Perhaps goals and objectives for each student, developed earlier from interests and needs, should be reconsidered if progress is not evident over time. Record keeping procedures discussed by Newman permit tracking an individual student's progress toward goals and such records are critical for evaluation. The records may show, for example, that the goals and objectives were inappropriate or that the strategies, organization, or resources should be reconsidered and changed. Evaluation is conducted to improve the effectiveness and efficiency of a project—not to declare something to be good or bad in an absolute sense. Every effort should be made to improve which frequently means revision.

Revision.

Newman stresses the need to be flexible when planning goals and objectives with students and deciding on materials, strategies, and type of organization. She insists the effective instructor is one who continually asks, "Is the learner achieving, at least to some extent, the goals and objectives you both agree upon" (p. 184)? She further suggests,

> Should the answers to any of these points be less than what you expected, you will have to reconsider various specifics: Were any of your instructional decisions arbitrary, too cumbersome to implement effectively, or poorly matched to your student's interests? If you can answer honestly and then

make the needed revisions, you will have gone a good way toward providing instruction that is meaningful, effective, and flexible (pp. 184–5).

Commentary

The literacy curriculum model proposed by Newman begins with an inventory of student needs and interests, develops goals and objectives from these needs and interests, and has a consideration of them influence subsequent decisions about instructional strategies, materials, organization, and evaluation. The language experience approach appears to be favored by Newman, but other reading approaches are discussed as possibilities from which instructors can choose or combine, depending on the needs of students as well as the instructor's particular style. With regard to strategies, the model is eclectic, not parochial.

The model is an example of a cooperative effort between teacher and student that permits negotiation over goals, means, and content. The emphasis on the student's interests suggests an openness and flexibility in curriculum planning that is quite different from the institutional model that presupposes group instruction. Obviously the attention to individual interests will likely be precluded if this model were to be used for group instructional purposes when the time and energy necessary for its implementation would be lacking.

Basic literacy involves certain skills of reading and writing, most of which could be specified with a great deal of precision, as are the objectives in the models for organizational effectiveness. Newman's treatment of this literacy model, however, demonstrates the importance she places on individual differences and the uniqueness of each learner. Her concern for the individual mollifies a preoccupation with terminal performance objectives, making this model a good example of an effort to reconcile education with training, one of the divergent problems that plague curriculum developers.

CHAPTER **6**

Freire's Literacy Model*

The model of literacy training promulgated by Freire and his followers is not in the form of step one, two, three, etc., but more in the form of criticism of conventional teaching and advocacy of educational ideas and methods that promote liberation. Freire is cited frequently in the adult education literature, not for his effectiveness in teaching illiterate adults how to read and write in forty hours, which he did (Bee, 1981), but because he set forth basic premises for working with adults that remain as challenges to adult educators everywhere.

Freire's method consists of using words for learning to read and write that come from the students. Three important criteria are: 1) the words are to be perceived by the students as representing important ideas or things with which the students are familiar, 2) the words have to have a phonetic value in representing the sounds of the langauge, and 3) whenever posible the words should have three syllables. Typically, "no more than 18 words were necessary for teaching adults to read and write syllabic, phonetic languages such as Portuguese and Spanish" (Bee, 1981, p. 44).

As Shaull indicates in the Foreword to Freire's *Pedagogy*, there is no

---

*A general outline of the model is contained in *Pedagogy of the Oppressed*, 1970, and *The Politics of Education*, 1985, as well as a discussion of the precepts on which the model is based. For more detailed information, one or both of these sources should be consulted.

point in trying to sum up, in a few pages, what Freire takes nearly
two hundred to say, but a few of the salient elements that undergird
his literacy model will be described below. The approach used here
will be to examine some of the assumptions Freire makes about education and how these assumptions affect implementation of the literacy model.

Freire considers domination to be a fundamental theme of the
times. Its opposite, liberation, is the overall goal toward which educators should work. Domination results in people being thought of
and treated as objects. Liberation requires people to think of themselves as subjects—actors who can influence their particular life situation and not just passively accept it. Through education for liberation
(pedagogy of the oppressed), people come to realize they are "in a
situation" and only as this situation ceases to be perceived as a "dense,
enveloping reality or tormenting blind alley" and they instead see it
as an "objective-problematic situation"—only then can they begin to
emerge from it because they can see how they can intervene in it.
Intervention, according to Freire, is "historical awareness itself . . . it
represents a step forward from emergence, and results from the *con-
scientizacão* . . . the deepening of the attitude of awareness characteristic of all emergence" (1970, pp. 100–101).

Freire's indictment of education, not just in Third World countries
but everywhere, is that it domesticates rather than liberates. Domesticating education treats people as objects, not subjects. Treatment as
objects, obviously, is dehumanizing. Freire's claim is that "the pedagogy of the oppressed is an instrument for their critical discovery that
both they and their oppressors are manifestations of dehumanization"
(1970, p. 33).

The teacher-student relationship that typifies conventional education is seen by Freire as being fundamentally narrative:

> This relationship involves a narrating subject (the teacher) and patient,
> listening objects (the students). The contents, whether values or empirical
> dimensions of reality, tend in the process of being narrated to become
> lifeless and petrified. Education is suffering from narration sickness (1970,
> p. 57).

By characterizing the teacher-student relationship as narration, Freire
introduces the idea of the "banking concept" of education.

> Instead of communicating, the teacher issues communiques and makes
> deposits which the students patiently receive, memorize, and repeat. . . . The

scope of the action allowed to the students extends only as far as receiving, filing, and storing the deposits (1970, p. 58).

The banking concept of education is to be avoided in the pedagogy of the oppressed and one way to avoid it is to conceive of teachers as learners and learners as teachers, creating, in effect, an education of equals, rather than an education that flows from the top down. The idea of teachers as learners is not just a conceptual convenience. Teachers must be learners as they begin their investigation of the people they intend to serve.

Whereas the "banking concept" was used to indict conventional education, generally, Freire (1985) considers typical approaches to adult literacy to be based on a "nutritionist concept," that means feeding and nourishing those hungry and starving for words. Only by returning to the idea of teachers as learners and learners as teachers can the "banking" and "nutritionist" metaphors be avoided.

Freire speaks of a team approach to literacy education. The team begins by recruiting volunteers who will help the team members learn as much as possible about the lives of the people who are illiterate. The team's approach is considered by Freire as an act of cultural synthesis, as opposed to cultural invasion.

> In cultural synthesis, the actors who come from "another world" to the world of the people do so not as invaders. They do not come to *teach* or *transmit* or to *give* anything, but rather to learn, with the people, about the people's world (1970, p. 181, emphasis in the original).

The temptation to avoid, in this inquiry, is to treat the people as objects, rather than subjects. The goal of the investigating team is to learn how the people view the world—"their concerns, their doubts, their hopes, their way of seeing the leaders, their perceptions of themselves and of the oppressors, their religious beliefs (almost always syncretic), their fatalism, their rebellious reactions" (1970, p. 184).

The investigative team that studies the area includes a psychologist and sociologist who assist in observing decoding of the codifications made during the investigation. The codification example Freire (1970 & 1985) uses is photographic slides that capture situations familiar to the participants. In addition to being familiar, Freire insists,

> an equally fundamental requirement for the preparation of the codifications is that their thematic nucleus be neither overly explicit nor overly enigmatic (1970, p. 107).

A picture too explicit may be seen as mere propaganda and therefore subject to slogans and one too enigmatic may be seen as a puzzle and become a guessing game.

The "investigation circle" that responds to the codifications should have a maximum of twenty participants. The number of such circles should be as many as are "necessary to involve, as participants, ten percent of the population of the area or subarea being served" (1970, p. 110). Once the codifications are initially discussed by participants, the interdisciplinary team listens to tape recordings of the sessions and analyzes the notes made by the psychologist and sociologist to find the themes that the codifications actually elicited among the participants. These themes, e.g., development, are then broken down in terms of "fundamental nuclei which, comprising learning units and establishing a sequence, give a general view of the theme" (1970, p. 113).

It may be discovered that certain predetermined themes are absent when the analysis is over. If so, the themes are included, even if they have not been suggested by the participants. Freire calls these "hinged themes" because they "facilitate the connection between two themes in the program unit, filling a possible gap between the two; or they may illustrate the relations between the general program content and the view of the world held by the people" (1970, p. 114). An example of a hinged theme is the anthropological concept of culture that "clarifies the role of men in the world and with the world as transforming rather than adaptive beings" (1970, p. 114).

After the themes are identified they are codified once again and may take various forms: slides, filmstrips, posters, etc. These materials will be used with culture circles to facilitate their learning to read and write and, in postliteracy projects, to become more politically literate. With regard to adult literacy, Freire (1985) offers an example of a lesson to illustrate the actual process and dialogue between teacher and participant.

> We shall describe in this appendix how a generative word from a syllabic language (in this case Partuguese) is decomposed, and how new words are formed from it.
> *Generative word*: a trisyllabic word chosen from the "linguistic universe" during research preliminary to the literacy course.
>   Example: *favela* "slum."
> *Codification*: the imaging of a significant aspect of a man's existential situation in a slum. The generative word is inserted in this codification. The codification functions as the knowable object mediating between the know-

ing subjects—the educator and learners—in the act of knowing they achieve in dialogue.

Real or concrete context: the slum reality as a framework for the objective facts that directly concern slum dwellers.

Theoretical context: the discussion group (*circulo de cultura*), in which the educators and learners—by means of the codification of the objective slum reality—engage in dialogue about the *reason* of the slum reality. The deeper this act of knowing goes, the more reality the learners unveil for what it is, discarding the myths that envelop it. This cognitive operation enables the learners to transform their interpretation of reality from mere opinion to a more critical knowledge.

Thus, as the theoretical context, the discussion group is the specialized environment where we submit the fact found in the concrete context, the slum, to critical analysis. The codification, representing those facts, is the knowable object. Decodification, breaking down the codified totality and putting it together again (retotalizing it), is the process by which the knowing subjects seek to know. The dialogical relationship is indispensable to this act.

Stages of Decodification: there are five stages.

(a) The knowing subjects begin the operation of breaking down the codified whole. This enables them to penetrate the whole in terms of the relationships among its parts, which until then the viewers did not perceive.

(b) After a thorough analysis of the existential situation of the slum, the semantic relation between the generative word and what it signifies is established.

(c) After the word has been seen in the situation, another slide is projected in which only the word appears, without the image of the situation: *favela.*

(d) The generative word is immediately separated into its syllables: *fa ve la.* The "family" of the first syllable is shown:

fa, fe, fi, fo, fu

Confronted with this syllabic family, the students identify only the syllable *fa*, which they know from the generative word. What is the next step for an educator who believes that learning to read and write is an act of knowing (who also knows that this is not, as for Plato, an act of remembering what has been forgotten)? He realizes that he must supply the students with new information, but he also knows that he must present the material to them as a problem. Thus, he poses two questions:

1. Do these "pieces" (the Brazilian students called the syllables pieces and there was no reason why they should be made to call them syllables) have something that makes them alike and something that makes them different?

2. At this moment, the educator asks another question: If they all begin the same way but end differently, can we call them all *fa?*

Again a brief silence; then, "No!"

Only at this point, having prepared the learners critically for the information, does the educator supply it. Since it was preceded by a problem, the information is not a mere gift.

Then comes the "family" of the words second syllable: *va, ve vi, vo, vu* The educator repeats the process. Some learners immediately say *va, ve, vi, vo vu.*

The "family" of the third syllable:

la, le, li, lo, lu

This slide is called the slide of discovery, a phrase coined by Professor Aurenice Cardoso, our assistant when we directed the National Plan for Adult Literacy in Brazil.

The educator proposes a horizontal and a vertical reading of the slide. This strengthens the learners' grasp of the vowel sounds *a, e, i, o, u.*

(e) Next, the educator asks the learners: Do you think we can (never, do you think *you* can) create something with these pieces?

This is the decisive moment for learning. It is the moment when those learning to read and write discover the syllabic composition of words in their langauge.

After a silence, sometimes disconcerting to the inexperienced educator, the learners begin, one by one, to discover the words of their language by putting together the syllables in a variety of combinations: *favela*, says one, *favo*, another; *fivela; luva; li; vale; vala; viva; falo; fale; fe; fava; vila; lava; vele; vela; vive; vivo; favala.*

With the second generative word, the learners combine its syllables not only among themselves but with those of the first word. Hence, knowing five or six generative words, the learners can begin to write brief notes. At the same time, however, they continue to discuss and critically analyze the real context as represented in the codifications.

This is what the primers cannot do. The authors of primers, as we have pointed out, choose generative words according to their own liking; they themselves decompose them; they themselves recombine their syllables to form new words; and with these words, they themselves evolve the phrases that generally echo the ones we have already quoted: *Eva viu a uva* ("Eva saw the grape"), *A asa é da ave* ("the birds wing") (1985, pp. 91–93. Emphasis in the original.).

The above lesson also demonstrates the opportunity the participants have to respond to both surface structure, which is descriptive, and deep structure, which involves understanding "the dialectic that exists between the categories presented in the surface structure, as well as the unity between the surface and deep structures" (1985, p. 52). Responding to a photographic slide of a cultural artifact, for example, a slum dwelling, the participants can describe the surface elements and begin to see that culture is "man-made," unlike trees and mountains. Being "man-made" means they can be (and have been) created and transformed by people. The deep structure in this case is the theme of transforming culture instead of always adapting to it.

The idea of cultural action is addressed by Freire in his discussion of praxis—the "authentic union of action and reflection" (1985, p. 87). Action without thought or reflection is mere activism to Freire, and thought without action is verbalization. It is the blend of thought and action and the cycle of enlightened thought, based on action and enlightened action, based on thought—praxis—that is needed by educators and participants in a pedagogy of the oppressed.

Again, two cautions must be noted. One is that no predetermined plan or model is suggested by Freire that would be mindlessly imposed on people. He suggests, for example, "Instead of following predetermined plans, leaders and people, mutually identified, together create the guidelines of their action" (1970, p. 183). The other caution, mentioned earlier, is that any attempt to condense or even summarize the profound ideas of Freire is subject to suspicion. The two primary sources listed at the beginning of this chapter should be consulted before a clear understanding of any of Freire's ideas can be assumed.

Commentary

Friere's emphasis on using words that originate with the learners < and consequently have greater meaning for the learners is the same technique employed by Ashton-Warner (1963) when she worked with Maori children in New Zealand. The method was not new with her, as she notes. What was and apparently still is new is the rejection of it. (Ashton-Warner, 1963, p. 28)

Commercial sources of basic word lists are not as necessary when using learners as sources for key vocabularies. With adults, however, the commercial interests may be combined with the political concerns that learners are becoming more sensitive to and active about their condition in the social order. Kozol (1981) for example, calls the learners' words dangerous. The danger is to the holders of power and those who represent the system as it is, i.e., the status quo.

This necessarily abbreviated treatment of Freire's injunctions regarding teaching adult literacy provides a bare minimum of understanding of basic precepts that undergird the model. It should be clear, however, that Freire's interests transcend education in the conventional sense and include the larger concern of culture, and specifically, cultural action. He sees illiteracy itself as "one of the concrete expressions of an unjust social reality" (1985, p. 10). His pedagogy "makes oppression and its causes objects of reflection by the oppressed, and from that reflection will come their necessary engagement in their struggle for their liberation" (1970, p. 33).

The process by which this pedagogy is implemented includes certain principles held inviolable. The conception of participants must be one of subjects or actors and not as objects. Teaching and learning are done with participants, who are never considered as empty vessels that need to be filled or linguistically or spiritually starving objects that need to be fed the word.

Although Freire has carried out most of his work in Brazil, Chile, Africa and other Third World countries, it is instructive to note that "his concept of the Third World is ideological and political rather than merely geographical" (Giroux, 1985 p. xviii). His contributions cannot be dismissed as irrelevant to countries outside the Third World. Indeed, he addresses head-on some of the persistent problems encountered in adult education. His use, for example, of "hinged themes" that are to be incorporated in a program even if they were not suggested by the participants, is an example of the compromise between simply responding to the expressed needs of learners and wholesale imposition of predetermined goals and expectations. And, as indicated in the brief discussion in the Introduction, such a compromise does not make the method less pure or less right, but simply reveals the value-based and action-based solution to a divergent problem.

Classifying this "model" as an example of an adult literacy curriculum model obviously does not do justice to the larger and intimately related purpose of liberation. But liberation, or elements thereof, can be detected as themes or concerns in other models as well. Learning more about Friere's model can provide insights into curriculum development. The degree to which a curriculum is planned cooperatively, where goals, methods, etc. are negotiated between educator and learner may be seen as the degree to which there is genuine concern for liberation as opposed to domestication.

SECTION IV

CONTINUING PROFESSIONAL EDUCATION

Many organized groups encourage or require their members to participate in educational activities. Continuing one's education in order to remain a member in good standing may be a harsh interpretation of why an adult who belongs to a group engages in an educational activity. A higher sounding reason for participation in continuing professional education is to keep abreast of changes in the field in order to improve the quality of services rendered.

Because of the variety of professions that provide or encourage continuing professional education, the treatment of this topic will begin in Chapter 7 with a set of guidelines developed by Houle (1980) that are applicable to many forms of curriculum models. His guidelines will be cast as an all-encompassing model against which specific models might be compared. Chapter 8 will focus on one specific example from the nursing profession to illustrate the application of Houle's guidelines within that profession's efforts at continuing education.

CHAPTER 7

Houle's Guidelines for Continuing Learning in the Professions*

Houle studied the continuing professional educational practices of seventeen types of professionals; accountants, architects, clergy, dentists, engineers, foresters, health care administrators, lawyers, librarians, military officers, nurses, pharmacists, physicians and surgeons, school administrators, teachers, social workers, and veterinarians. His insights into continuing professional education are considered here as guidelines for developing curriculum models. His earlier work, *The Design of Education* (1972), addresses a generic model of curriculum that could accommodate the guidelines in this present effort.

It may be too that the emphasis on learning, as opposed to education (seen in the comparison of titles of Houle's 1972 and 1980 books) reflects the realization that adults may well be learning without the benefit of an educator's plans, or even without conscious realization on the learner's part. Continuing learning in the professions is taking place, and much of it, to be sure, is the result of educational plans intended to promote leaning, but Houle sees other kinds of learning

---

*For a more detailed description of these guidelines, see Houle's *Continuing Learning in the Professions*, 1980. Unless otherwise indicated, all references within this chapter will be from this source.

occurring in the professions. His view is that of a third party; one who observes the activities and reports them within a general framework that can be considered a model for educational designers who wish to improve the opportunities for learning among the professionals they serve.

The conventional conception of continuing education, according to Houle, was a relatively undifferentiated series of attempts to maintain or modernize the professional's knowledge and skill that occurred after induction into the profession. The modern conception of continuing professional education reflects anticipated events in the career span of the professional. Figure 7.1 depicts the typical stages of a professional's career and the placement of continuing professional education with regard to those stages.

It is important to remember that instead of focusing on a particular way in which continuing professional education can and should serve the various professions, Houle has taken a macroview of all kinds of continuing education with regard to their appropriateness to the many aspects of groups seeking increased professionalization. His comprehensive treatment of continuing professional education provides a framework, into which any number of curriculum models could fit.

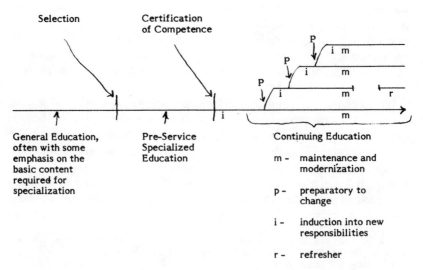

Figure 7.1   *An Emerging Model of Professional Education (Houle, 1980, p.106).*

Three Modes of Learning

Houle divides all the possible ways individuals learn within professional settings into "three major and overlapping modes of learning" (p. 31). The modes are inquiry, instruction, and performance.

Inquiry. "The mode of inquiry is the process of creating some new synthesis, idea, technique, policy, or strategy of action" (p. 31). Wherever professionals, working alone or in groups, investigate a new idea they are involved in the process of inquiry. The activity may be formalized and structured, as in the instances of seminars or clinics, or it may be informal in the sense that the learning is a by-product "of efforts directed primarily at establishing policy, seeking consensus, working out compromises, and projecting plans" (p. 31).

The chief characteristic of inquiry is that although the process through which it operates may be planned, its outcomes cannot be predicted. Houle notes, for example, that didacticism, a process wherein certain objectives are predetermined, is a blight to the mode of inquiry. He does not rule out the possibility that one could attend a lecture in order to enhance the inquiry, but that the overall process is negated if the activities result in accomplishing predetermined objectives.

Instruction. When the objectives are known in advance and an activity is designed for the learners to achieve the objectives, the entire process is called instruction. Conventional schooling is based almost entirely on the instructional mode. Because of the frequency of its use, conventional wisdom equates instruction with education. Houle does not dispute the popularity and importance of instruction as a mode of learning. He tries to broaden, however, the conception of continuing professional education to include other modes of learning, namely inquiry and performance.

Performance. "The mode of performance is the process of internalizing an idea or using a practice habitually, so that it becomes a fundamental part of the way in which a learner thinks about and undertakes his or her work" (p. 32). Performance may include some prerequisite learning, either through inquiry or instruction, but it is considered separately because it is such a critical part of the entire process of continuing professional education. Regardless of what is learned through the modes of inquiry and instruction, if a professional does not incorporate the newly acquired knowledge, skill, or sensitivity in his or her behavior, the impact of the educational effort is nil. Unlike inquiry or instruction, effective performance may be achieved by adjustments that are external to the learner. Changing regulations or rewards may be necessary before changes in performance can be observed.

Houle suggests the three modes of learning have not been made as conceptually distinctive as they might be. He insists that they are different enough in terms of principles that ought to guide their effective use that the three modes and their attendant principles should be utilized more imaginatively, in continuing professional education than they have in the past.

Five Basic Settings for Professional Practice

Just as there is more than one mode of learning, Houle reminds there is more than one setting in which professionals practice. The different settings create different needs and continuing professional education, if is to be effective, should be sensitive to the distinctive features of each of the settings.

Enterpreneurial. An entrepreneurial setting is one in which the professional offers direct service to the client. The professional may work alone or in partnership with colleagues, but takes personal responsibility for organizing and operating the practice.

Collective. A group of like professionals who share in setting goals and organizing the practice is called a collective. A staff of librarians or social workers within an organization are examples of a collective.

Hierarchical. A work setting wherein the central mission is the same as the profession, but the professionals perform at different levels of authority. A school system with a superintendent, principal, and teachers is an example of a hierarchical setting.

Adjunct. A work setting wherein a professional's practice is different from the central mission of the institution is considered an adjunct setting. An attorney in the employ of a business firm is professional service in an adjunct capacity.

Facilitative. Whenever a professional works in a setting designed to promote the progress of the profession itself, that professional is said to be working in a facilitative setting. Publishing houses, foundations, and research bureaus are examples of facilitative settings.

The five settings Houle discusses can be interwoven. For example, a group of English teachers can represent a collective within a school or system, but also are part of a hierarchical setting. The time is past, according to Houle, when those responsible for continuing professional education can assume all professionals work in the same kinds of settings and face similar needs. By differentiating the various work settings, Houle calls attention to the need for assorted educational experiences that may be appropriate for each. Combined with the three modes of learning—inquiry, instruction, and performance— the five primary work settings begin to represent the complexity of continuing professional education. Adding to the mix of factors that can constitute continuing professional education is the variety of providers.

Houle discusses seven dominant providers—autonomous groups, associations, professional schools, universities, employment settings, independent providers, and purveyors of professional supplies and equipment (pp. 167–192). Descriptions of providers are not critical to the standards Houle discusses for continuing professional education, hence they will be passed over here in order to move on to the characterisitcs of professionalization, which Houle claims should be the goals for continued learning in the professions.

Fourteen Characteristics of Professionalization

The characteristics of professionalization Houle discusses reflect the dynamic nature of the concept. This dynamic quality is in contrast to the static denotation of the term professionalism. Any vocation wanting to become more professional must attend to the dynamic characteristics of professionalization. The goal is not to achieve some ideal state, once and for all, but to continue to strive for goals that lie outside their reach. Houle asserts:

> The needs of society require that every professionalizing occupation become better than it is, and at least part of the effort it must exert is the improvement of its pattern of lifelong learning. A dynamic concept of professionalization offers educators both the opportunity and the challenge to use active principles of learning to help achieve the basic aims of the group with which they work (p. 30).

The once widely held notion that there is a charmed circle of professions has given way to a new perspective. Houle claims:

> Every occupation that is called a profession is, in reality, a semiprofession. The analysis of an occupation can assess its degree of professionalization in terms of the number and quality of performance of characteristics chosen as essential (p. 28).

After studying seventeen different professionalizing groups, Houle suggests there are fourteen essential characteristics, all but one of which is a candidate, alone or in combination with others, for a goal or objective in continuing professional education.

Clarifying its defining function or functions. New recruits to a profession may have chosen that profession based on a nonexpert view of its central mission. Within the professional school, however, it may become obvious that there are conflicting views of what the primary function of the profession should be. Leaders in the field also may not agree in their definitions of the function of a profession. This relative instability of mission, purpose, or function is especially evident, according to Houle, in the fields of architecture, pharmacy, and dentistry (pp. 36-38).

Whatever the cause for the disagreement regarding the definition of function, the practitioners need to expect "to be constantly challenged by the assertion of new fundamental orientations and in all cases the three modes of education . . . may become operative" (p. 39). The process of discussion and debate over a challenge to a central mission would be indicative of the inquiry mode of learning. Consistent with the inquiry process, the specific outcome would be unknown until the process is terminated. But the termination would be tentative, because of the dynamic quality of the characteristics associated with professionalization.

If some kind of closure is achieved, albeit tentative, dissemination of the results of inquiry would reflect the instruction mode of learning. And consistent with the mode of instruction, predetermined objectives would be used. Instructional activities would be planned around the objectives. The intent would be to achieve the objectives through didactic or other forms of the instructional mode.

Once the objectives are determined, as a result of inquiry, and disseminated through instruction, the final phase is performance—"the adoption of the new mission as an internalized and habitually used concept" (p. 39). Houle warns, "adoption of a new unifying concept is never easy, particularly if it requires a complete reorientation of practice" (p. 39). Effective integration into practice may require changes in policy and regulation. Monitoring changes in performance may be done by peers, colleagues, or one's self. The performance mode of learning is consequently different from inquiry and instruction in terms of objectives, process, and results.

Whenever an occupational field actively seeks to redefine or reestablish its basic functions, the individual practitioners can be expected to participate in all three modes of learning. The inquiry mode may only be engaged in by a relatively small number, but once a settlement is reached, the instructional and performance modes should involve all members of the occupational group. Those who plan continuing professional educational activities need to be aware of opportunities to initiate or facilitate the learning experiences in all three modes. The remaining thirteen characteristics of professionalization will be briefly presented below. The applicability of the three modes of learning for each characteristic should be apparent.

Mastery of theoretical knowledge. Every occupational field seeking professionalization is based on theoretical knowledge contained in the disciplines of the arts and sciences (p. 40). This knowledge base is in contrast to the practical or applied knowledge contained in many professional preparation programs. Theoretical knowledge in ethics, for example, is different from legal ethics that may be taught in a law school. Psychology, likewise, is different from educational psychology. The disciplines within the arts and sciences are seeking truth in contrast to the applied fields wherein solutions to individual or social problems are pursued.

Returning to the study of disciplines that undergird the practice of an occupation is not unusual. Houle maintains the extent to which "practitioners take advantage of their opportunities to acquire basic knowledge, their professionalization is broadened" (p. 42).

Capacity to solve problems. Houle claims, "The ultimate test of the success of a professional is the ability to solve problems (or to decide that they cannot be solved), and those problems usually involve vital and deeply significant outcomes" (p. 43). Houle further claims that frequent encounters with common problems begin to work against maintaining a critical sensitivity to them. Routine can lead to boredom and dullness. Continued learning is no guarantee of preventing burnout in the practitioner, but sensitivity to the need practitioners have to solve problems can help designers of continuing professional education plan programs that address this need.

Use of practical knowledge. Rooted in the theory-based disciplines, the practical knowledge is that which applies directly to the occupation. Appearing in professional schools with such course titles as legal ethics or educational psychology, these new disciplines are geared to solving individual and social problems through the application of theories or tenets developed over time within the profession. Using one's own experience to increase knowledge and skill fits in this category, as well. This combination of new knowledge from the applied fields with the practitioners' experiences usually results in enlightened practice.

Self-enhancement. Including and acting upon interests other than one's occupation is what Houle considers efforts toward self-enhancement. Becoming too specialized is as dangerous to full development of an individual as never specializing at all. One's capacity for learning is enlarged when other interests are maintained and, conversly, when specialization excludes from the life of the mind other intellectual interests, it can be destructive of the whole person. Houle has observed that even when the professional field itself makes no provision for this enhancement, many practitioners discover on their own that developing new interests can provide valuable insights to their practice.

Formal training. With few exceptions, the occupations seeking professionalization see to it that "formal procedures should be established to transmit the essential body of knowledge and technique of the vocation to all recognized practitioners before they enter service and throughout their careers" (p. 51). Although colleges and universities seem to have a corner on the market for providing such formal training, other institutions, such as hospitals, industries, or associations are providing preparatory as well as continuing education for some professions. Regardless of the source, formal training is seen as an indispensable characteristic of professionalization.

Credentialing. The evolution from individualized and unregulated practice to modern professionalism, according to Houle, was facilitated by the recognition of the need for formal credentialing (p. 54). Credentialing is typically carried out by state government. It is the formal means by which an individual's capacity to perform at an acceptable level is tested.

Advanced credentialing is usually the responsibility of associations that may include requirements for further study, internship, and examination. Examples of this kind of additional licensure abound in medicine. Credentialing, provisional, standard, or advanced, is based on education and training, including, specifically continuing professional education. Learning more about credentialing itself may be legitimate content for continuing professional education.

Creation of a subculture. Creating a subculture means promoting "lore, folkways, mores, traditions, role differentiations and relationships, variations in authority and power, personal prestige systems, language and special references not understood by the uninitiated, and clusterings of people with distinctive functions" (p. 57). Most of the immersion into this subculture is achieved informally, according to Houle, but it can be promoted through continuing professional education planned and carried out by members of the subculture. Too much acculturation can become dysfunctional or at least run counter to other characteristics, such as self-enhancement. To guard against possible negative effects of the subculture some professions hire individuals from other specialities to carry out their continuing professional education. Continuing legal education and continuing nursing education, for example, are oftentimes directed by specialists from adult education or university extension centers.

Legal reinforcement. A professionalizing occupation often needs the force of law to protect the special rights and privileges of its practitioners. Houle notes, "among these prerogatives are the exclusive right to practice their profession, the power to perform legally binding acts, the right to maintain inviolable confidentiality in their relationships with their clients, and access to financial support for their research and training activities" (p. 59).

It is not unusual for states to require specific preparation as well as continuing education for many occupations. The efforts to influence law-making bodies regarding special rights or privileges frequently affect the content of continuing professional education programs. Even at the preparation stage of professional training, the current issues involving special cases of law that are unique to an occupational group are studied. But the greater impact is at the continuing education level when the inquiry mode may be used to pursue understanding, resolution, or consensus regarding a legal issue; the instructional mode is used to disseminate information about the issue or to persuade others regarding a point of view; and the performance mode is used to regulate or monitor, by others or one's self, the changes in practice the law effects.

Public acceptance. Critical to any professionalizing occupation is public acceptance of it as a profession. Houle reviews a number of studies of public acceptance (pp. 61–63) and concludes that many occupational groups have increased the awareness of the public of the nature of their work, but that relative ranking among many groups has remained virtually unchanged over time. Unlike any of the other thirteen characteristics, Houle believes public acceptance should not be addressed directly through continuing education, but should be expected to improve as a by-product of other educational emphases.

Ethical practice. Establishing and maintaining a tradition of ethical practice is important to the continued esteem enjoyed by an occupational group. Houle considers one of the greatest challenges to continuing education to be establishing settings where the ethical issues can be debated and discussed. And, as is the case with so many of the other characteristics, all three modes of learning are used when considering, disseminating, and applying resolutions of ethical issues.

Penalties. Failure to act according to accepted standards of ethical practice should result in penalties to the individuals of an occupational group if that group is concerned with advancing its professionalization. Continuing professional education should address the application of ethical standards to promote this characteristic of professionalization.

Relations to other vocations. A built-in tension exists between practitioners of different, but related occupational groups. Because each group is seeking to stake out its territory of practice and become more autonomous, it is inevitable that closely allied groups may perceive one another as adversaries. Houle believes amelioration of present separation is possible and advisable for the mutual benefit of the affected groups. Continuing professional education can serve to improve relations with other vocations by using team approaches in employment settings and by providing training opportunities that require collaborative approaches.

Relations to users of service. Houle claims only the simpler forms of relationships can be learned in preprofessional training and that usually the subtler and more complex aspects of the relations to users of a service can be learned only through experience. Continuing education can facilitate this understanding through the three modes of learning available to practitioners.

The fourteen characteristics of professionalization can never be fully achieved and, as Houle points out, "the race for professional accomplishment has no finish line" (p. 74). Overall, these fourteen characteristics should constitute the goals for vocations seeking increased professionalization. Continuing professional education can assist each individual practitioner in his or her effort to become more professional.

Commentary

Houle's study of seventeen vocational groups, combined with his extensive experience in continuing professional education, have yielded a number of generalizations that are offered as guides to developing more specific models of curriculum. His macroapproach to continuing professional education permits generalizations across many different vocational groups. The two generalizations that have the most importance for individuals developing curricula for professional continuing education are the dynamic conception of professionalization and the three modes of learning used by practitioners in a vocational group.

Moving from the static notion of achieving professional status, once and for all, Houle conceives continuous activity by practitioners to improve themselves, as well as the larger group, to be the reality of continuing learning in the professions. The new conception is dynamic and consequently, requires continuous adjustment by curriculum directors who serve the vocational groups. The movement toward professionalization not only will never end (there "is no finish line"), but needs the assistance of curriculum planners who know this and understand their facilitative role in the overall process of professionalization. A clarification of this facilitative role is the second important lesson Houle provides the curriculum planner.

Expanding the conception of learning from one mode to three, Houle creates new opportunities for curriculum planners to make their educational plans more appropriate to the actual learning taking place. Whereas instruction has been the mainstay of most continuing professional education practices, Houle's recognition of inquiry and performance as legitimate learning modes opens up new possibilities for at least recognizing if not planning for educational experiences that capitalize on all three modes of learning. Appropriate curriculum models for continuing education in the professions will have to not only create access to knowledge, as in the conventional mode of instruction, but anticipate helping individuals gain access, as in the mode of inquiry. Efforts to help with self-monitoring of actual practice should be seen as legitimate activities for continuing educators. Broadening the view of education to accommodate three modes of learning means curriculum workers will have to reexamine their programs and adjust them to meet demands, anticipate needs, and generally be more useful to the groups they serve.

CHAPTER 8

Continuing Education in Nursing

In the previous chapter an overview of continuing professional education, based on Houle's analysis (1980), was provided. After surveying and studying seventeen occupations that are involved in the process of professionalization, Houle discussed three modes of learning (inquiry, instruction, and performance) common to professionals continuing their education and thirteen characteristics of professionalization that he claims as appropriate goals for continuing professional education. Houle's contribution will be the backdrop against which the American Nurses' Association's guidelines and standards for continuing education in nursing will be described.*

Overview

The American Nurses' Association (ANA), the professional organization for nurses, has developed a philosophy of continuing education in nursing (1984), standards for continuing education in nursing (1984), guidelines and models for staff development (1976,

---

*Sources for guidelines, standards, and models include: *Guidelines for Staff Development* (1976, rev. 1978), Kansas City: American Nurses' Association (ANA); *Self-Directed Continuing Education in Nursing* (1978), Kansas City: ANA; *Continuing Education in Nursing: An Overview* (1979), Kansas City: ANA; and *Standards for Continuing Education in Nursing* (1984), Kansas City: ANA.

rev. 1978) and guidelines for self-directed continuing education in nursing (1978). These materials, by definition, are general and intended as guides in developing or assessing specific continuing education practices. A certain amount of flexibility in application is assumed, but general intent can be inferred from them. In the interest of consistency of communication, each publication contains a glossary of terms relevant to the specific topic of the publication as well as to continuing education in nursing generally.

The ANA assists the state nurses' associations in developing continuing education approval and recognition programs that, in turn, can approve continuing education efforts at the local level. The guidelines and standards published by the ANA must be met if a state or local organization seeks accreditation for its offerings of continuing professional education.

Definitions and Descriptions

The conception of continuing education upon which the ANA bases its standards and guidelines is depicted in Figure 8.1. The overlap between continuing education and staff development reflects the ambiguity occasionally associated with the terms. The ANA offers definitions and descriptions to differentiate among them. The ANA broadly defines continuing education as "a lifelong learning process that builds on and modifies previously acquired knowledge, skills, and attitudes" (ANA, 1979, p. v). The basic unit of measurement for continuing education in nursing is the contact hour—"50 minutes of an approved, organized learning experience" (1979, p. 3). Ten contact hours represent one continuing education unit (CEU). The CEU has been defined as ten contact hours "in an organized, non-credit continuing education experience under responsible sponsorship, capable direction, and qualified instruction" (National Task Force on the Continuing Education Unit, n.d., as quoted in ANA, 1979, p. 3).

Continuing education "consists of those planned educational activities intended to build upon the educational and experiential bases of the professional nurse for the enhancement of practice, education, administration, research, or theory development to the end of improving the health of the public" (1984, p. 5). The content for continuing education can include "current and emerging concepts, principles, practices, theories, and/or research in or related to nursing" (1984, p. 5). The definition and content of continuing education are bounded only by the general field of nursing and areas related

CONTINUING EDUCATION

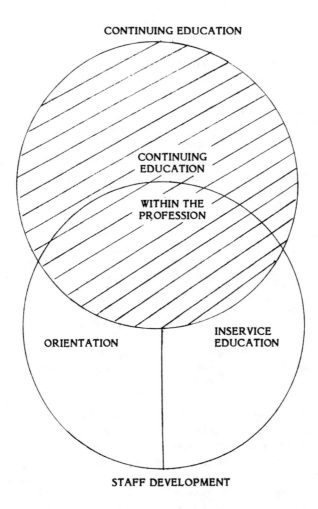

CONTINUING
EDUCATION

WITHIN THE
PROFESSION

ORIENTATION

INSERVICE
EDUCATION

STAFF DEVELOPMENT

Figure 8.1 *Relation Between Continuing Education and Staff Development (ANA, 1984, p. 6).*

to nursing. Staff development is bound, however, by the interests and concerns of the employing organization.

Staff development, according to the ANA, "is a process consisting of orientation, inservice education, and continuing education for the purpose of promoting the development of personnel within any employment setting consistent with the goals and responsibilities of the employer" (1984, p. 5). Orientation serves to introduce new employees to the organization or to introduce established employees to new roles and responsibilities. Inservice education, as another part of staff development, "consists of activities intended to assist the professional nurse to acquire, maintain, and/or increase competence in fulfilling the assigned responsibilities specific to the expectations of the employer" (p. 5). Staff developmnent, because it is defined as being bounded by expectations of the employer, can be seen as a set of activities designed to improve organizational effectiveness. Conflict between the ANA's purposes and an employer's purposes are possible. The standards reveal a cognizance of the possibility, but no remedy for reconciling is offered.

Standards

The ANA indirectly addresses this issue of purpose under its first standard:

> Overall organization and administration of the continuing education provider unit *are consistent with the sponsoring agency's stated philosophy, purpose, and goals,* are compatible with the American Nurses' Association's standards of nursing education, nursing practice, and continuing education (1984, p. 7, emphasis added).

The potential problem of the continuing education unit within an organization being in conflict with the organization's philosophy, purpose, or goals is not addressed directly. The implication appears to be that those responsible for continuing education will arrange, somehow, to be consistent with the sponsoring agency's philosophy, purpose, and goals. Serving two masters, however, can be difficult. The ANA's primary goal, as stated in its philosophy, is to maintain and improve the health of the public (1984, p. 3). Ideally, health care organizations have the same goals, but also work within finite budgets that may create occassions when the organization's needs are at cross purposes with the profession's. It is apparently left to the resourcefulness of the director of continuing education to mediate any differences if they emerge.

Standard 2, "Human Resources" speaks to the qualifications of the director of continuing education, faculty, resource persons, and support staff. The director should be a nurse with at least a master's degree "who is knowledgeable regarding adult learning principles" (1984, p. 8). Under the heading of process criteria, the ANA suggests the director and faculty should engage in self-evaluation, incorporate concepts of adult learning principles in teaching, collaborate with other nurses and members of other health care fields to meet learning needs of the target audience, possess expertise in the content to be taught, and have competence in teaching the assigned content. (1984, pp. 8–9.

Standard 3 is the "Learner." It is recommended, under this standard, that the registered nurse learners participate in determining their own learning needs and planning the continuing education activities. The continuing education unit is expected to provide mechanisms whereby learners can assess their own needs, contribute to the planning of continuing education activities, and participate in the evaluation of same.

Standard 4 is the "Educational Design." The design "consists of planned, organized, and evaluated learning experiences based on the principles of adult learning" (1984, p. 10). Under the heading of process criteria, the ANA outlines the developmental steps for design.

Through the educational design the provider
1. assesses learning needs of the target audience.
2. plans continuing activities which reflect identified needs of the target population.
3. states behavioral objectives for each continuing education program.
4. selects content for each continuing program in relation to objectives.
5. relates content to nursing knowledge or nursing practice.
6. selects teaching methods for each continuing education program in relation to objectives, content, and principles of adult learning.
7. ensures availability of adequate resources, including qualified faculty, to implement each continuing education program.
8. develops evaluation strategies for each continuing education program in relation to objectives and to principles of adult learning (1984, pp. 10–11).

An amplification of what is meant by principles of adult learning appears under the heading of outcome criteria:

The educational design operationalizes principles of adult learning
   a. The learner is represented in identifying learning needs.
   b. Content is relevant to an identified need.

  c. Teaching strategies experientially involve the learner.
  d. The learner participates in the evaluation process (1984, p. 11).

Also included under outcome criteria is a succinct description of design: "The design for each continuing education program includes a needs assessment, behavioral objectives, content outline, teaching methods, learning experiences, resource utilization plan, and evaluation strategies" (1984, p. 11).

The description of design appears to accommodate what Houle (1980) calls the instruction mode. Inquiry and performance, the other two learning modes Houle observed professionals using, do not come readily to mind when the outcome criteria regarding design are encountered. Inquiry as a mode of learning appears to be legitimized in that guidelines and criteria for self-directed continuing education have been published by the ANA (1978), but more about self-directed learning later. The standard for design clearly anticipates a group instructional process.

The succeeding three standards deal with resources and facilities, records and reports, and evaluation. Only evaluation will be examined here because it reveals a broadening of scope in terms of legitimate goals for continuing education.

In addition to the standard requiring evaluation be an "integral, ongoing, and systematic quality assurance process" (1984, p. 13), the structure criteria include "quality assurance mechanisms . . . to determine the effectiveness of individual programs in achieving *cognitive, affective, and/or behavioral changes* in the learner . . ." (1984, p. 13, emphasis added). Whereas, under design it was indicated that behavioral objectives were to be written for each program, the evaluation standard appears to create the possibility that objectives other than behavioral ones are legitimate. If, however, it is intended that all objectives are to be behavioral some torturous efforts will have to be expended to accommodate the implied criterion of behaviorism within cognitive and especially affective goal categories.

Also under the evaluation standard the outcome criteria include, "When feasible, evaluation data provide evidence that the learner incorporated in nursing practice the knowledge, skills, and attitudes acquired through continuing education programs" (1984, p. 14). This criterion reflects Houle's performance mode of learning, i.e., the actual implementation of new techniques, approaches etc. in the professional practice. It must be noted, however, that this performance criterion is within a context that suggests it as a natural extension of a program design as opposed to Houle's conception of it being a legitimate continuing education activity in and of itself.

Guidelines for Staff Development

A staff development program provides orientation, inservice education, and, when the goals exceed the needs and interests of a specific employer, continuing education. "The primary goal of a nursing staff development program is to provide opportunities for employed nursing personnel to acquire further knowledge, skills, and attitudes necessary to perform their assigned functions safely and effectively in the provision of health care for consumers" (ANA, 1976, 1978, p. 2).

As indicated earlier, staff development includes orientation for new employees or those established employees facing new responsibilities, inservice education that enhances current levels of performance, and continuing education for which the purpose is twofold: 1) to improve current performance on the job and 2) to increase current knowledge and improve performance that would be applicable in other job settings as well. The continuing education portion of staff development will be examined more closely because "only activities in the continuing education component qualify for the continuing education contact hour" (1976, 1978, p. 2).

In order to qualify for the contact hour, ten of which equal one continuing education unit (CEU), the educational design of an offering should include:

* Behavioral objectives
* Content, teaching strategies, and evaluation methods which relate to the objectives
* Qualified faculty
* Appropriate learning facilities (1976, 1978, p. 2).

The variety of activities of continuing education include "workshops, conferences, seminars, institutes, courses, and self-directed learning in which achievement will be evaluated" (1976, 1978, p. 2).

The steps in developing a staff development program are outlined in Figure 8.2. Step 6, "Identify needs" is the beginning point for curriculum development per se. The inclusion of organizational needs makes it evident that staff development is indeed a model similar to the one described in the first chapter; Nadler's Critical Events Model,

1. Develop a philosophy
    A. Define staff development
    B. Determine purpose of staff development

2. Develop and determine program goals, including short- and long-range objectives

3. Determine and define components

4. Determine policies

5. Determine organizational structure
    A. Determine human resources needed
    B. Identify roles, responsibilities, and accountability of department personnel
    C. Establish communication system

6. Identify needs
    A. Assess organizational needs
    B. Assess group needs
    C. Assess individual needs
    D. Establish priorities

7. Formulate objectives
    A. Write general educational objectives
    B. Write general learner objectives

8. Determine program evaluation
    A. Establish system for collecting, organizing, and reporting data
    B. Develop evaluation tools

9. Determine physical and material resources needed
    A. Identify hardware and software needed
    B. Determine class and conference room space needed
    C. Determine needed office space
    D. Identify library needs

10. Develop a record keeping system

11. Prepare budget

12. Determine schedule of activities
    A. Identify dates of employment by category of employee (registered nurse, licensed practical nurse, nurse's aide, etc.)
    B. Identify specific courses, conferences, etc., based on priorities of need

13. Communicate plan to significant others

14. Implement program

15. Evaluate program
    A. Collect evaluative data
    B. Organize evaluative data
    C. Report evaluative data

16. Revise program as indicated

Figure 8.2   *Steps in Program Development (ANA, 1976, 1978, p. 13).*

for which the primary purpose was achieving organizational effectiveness. The nursing staff development model appears to be an institutional model that is also a cooperative one in that needs and interests of the organization and the professionalizing group have to be negotiated.

Self-Directed Continuing Education in Nursing

Throughout the standards and guidelines published by the ANA the individual nurse's responsibility for assessing needs and taking action to address them is evident. Specific attention to self-directed continuing education in nursing is contained in the document by the same title (ANA, 1978). Self-directed education may be especially appropriate for nurses who are geographically or professionally isolated and unable to attend traditional continuing education functions and/or those for whom the traditional functions are inappropriate in terms of learning styles. If a nurse engages in self-directed education and wants recognition for it, the suggestions published by ANA or the individual's state association should be followed. The structure suggested by ANA is done in the interest of establishing some uniformity regarding what could otherwise be unique experiences. The uniformity is necessary for facilitating interstate transfer of continuing education records.

A self-directed learning activity can take many forms and include a wide range of activities, as will become evident in a more detailed description of it in Section VI, Chapters 10 and 11. The ANA (1978) defines a self-directed learning activity as "one for which the learner takes the initiative and responsibility for the learning process" (p. 2). The process includes control over the following learning variables:

- Identification of learning needs
- Topic and purpose of the learning activity
- Objectives or expected outcomes
- Appropriate learning experiences
- Learning resources
- Environment
- Time
- Place
- Methods of evaluation
- Methods of documentation (ANA, 1978, p. 2)

Examples of self-designed activities, wherein the learner controls a majority of the variables, could include individual reading projects and independent learning projects. When the learner controls a limited number of the variables, the activity is considered other-designed and could include activities such as a correspondence course, directed reading, and programmed instruction.

The essential steps of the self-designed process are: Planning, Implementation, Evaluation, and Documentation (ANA, 1978, pp. 3-5).

Planning. The planning step includes identifying learning needs, which may be done by the individual or by the individual's supervisor. A decision must be made at this stage regarding which, if any, of the learning needs can be met through self-directed study. Goals and priorities also should be determined at this stage.

The next planning step is the selection of specific focus for the learning project. It is recommended the focus be related to professional competence and needed practice. A statement of purpose for the project should be developed. This statement would address the question, "Why is this project being undertaken?"

The third topic within the planning step is detemination of expected outcome objectives.

> The expected outcomes are expressed as objectives for the learner. The objectives should be measurable, attainable, and more specific than the statement of purpose (ANA, 1978, p. 4).

Examples of objectives are not provided, but the criterion of measurability implies behavioral or performance objectives would be appropriate.

Assessing and selecting learning resources is another part of the planning step. Audio-visual materials, including tapes, television, and professional literature, are among the variety listed as material resources. Human resources could include allied health professionals, colleagues, and librarians (ANA, 1978, p. 4).

Determining methods of evaluation is the next step in planning a self-directed activity. The types of objectives, the availability of resources, and preference of the learner will affect the decision of what type(s) of evaluation will be appropriate.

Also during the planning step, attention should be given to the procedure that will be used to document the self-directed activity. This documentation may be an extension of the evaluation method chosen earlier. The ANA offers several examples of documentation:

1. A written research or other professional paper, with or without reviewer's comments.
2. A letter of acceptance for publication from a professional journal.
3. Written verification of successful mastery of a clinical skill. Verification by an expert in the field may be needed, if the approval body requests it.
4. An annotated bibliography.
5. Successful completion of a written exam prepared by an expert in the field.
6. Written case study with or without reviewer's comments. (If previously accepted as a part of ANA's certification process, a copy of the notification of certification is acceptable). (1978, pp. 4–5).

The examples illustrate the need for planning exactly what kind of documentation will be used. The concern is that there be "tangible evidence that objectives have been achieved" (1978, p. 4).

The final consideration listed under the planning step is an estimate of the amount of time the learning activity will take. Overall completion time (hours, days, weeks, or months) is estimated in order to aid day-to-day scheduling of time, but actual contact hours should be estimated in order to convert the project into CEU's, the basic currency of continuing education.

Implementation. Putting the plan to work may require changes in the original intentions. The suggestion is that such changes be noted in the final report, along with the rationale for the changes, and that the learner need not renegotiate with the approval agency. (ANA, 1978, p. 5)

Evaluation. Formative evaluation occurs as the learning project proceeds. Formative evaluation enables the learner to judge the relevance to purpose and objectives of any of the materials used or activities experienced. The purpose and objectives themselves could be adjusted as the result of formative evaluation. Summative evaluation occurs at the end of the learning project and is an assessment of how well the objectives were met.

Documentation. When the learning project is completed, the procedure chosen for documentation (see the six examples above) is included in the final report of the project to the approval agency. The actual number of contact hours is reported as part of the documentation step.

Criteria for Approval of a Self-Designed Continuing Education Product

The ANA suggests criteria for state approval boards of state nurses' associations or state licensure boards. The criteria correspond with each of the steps described above and serve, in effect, to assure that each step was taken with full realization of what the step represented. For example, regarding learner's needs, evidence is required that the proposed "project is based on the individual's identification of her own learning needs" (1978, p. 6). Even if a supervisor initially identified the need, the implication is that the learner at least recognize it as legitimate. Also with regard to the learner's needs, the criterion of being realistic is to be applied to the self-directed project as an appropriate method for meeting the needs of the learner.

Focus of the project includes several criteria. The title of the project must reflect a specific area of concentration. The purpose statement should "describe the relationship of the content of the project to the learner's professional practice and competence or to the bodies of knowledge that contribute to nursing practice" (1978, p. 6). It is expected that there be an overview of the project in the description of it as well as how the specific project is related to the learner's long range goals.

The criteria for objectives are:

1. The objectives are clearly stated.
2. The objectives appear to be attainable in the proposed time.
3. The objectives are measurable.
4. The objectives indicate learner outcomes (1978, p. 6).

The clear implication is that the objectives are predetermined and behavioral.

Criteria for resources and learning experiences include appropriateness and adequacy. The resources and experiences must relate to the objectives of the learner.

Evaluation criteria are that the method of evaluation must be planned and be appropriate for the objectives being sought. Overlapping evaluation is documentation, the sole criterion for which is that a plan for it must be described.

Finally, the estimated time schedule should be evaluated in terms of overall length (hours, days, weeks, months) being realistic as well as specific contact hour estimates being appropriate for the proposed project.

The suggestions for the self-directed project and the criteria against which the steps of the process can be judged, are intended as guides (1978, p. 3) and approval bodies apparently have some latitude in interpretation.

Commentary

Although some commentary has been included throughout the description of the ANA's models for continuing professional education, a few additional remarks will be offered here. The description of Houle's (1980) observations will be the point of departure.

Regarding goals and content of continuing professional education, it appears as if the ANA's standards and guidelines do not limit what could be considered legitimate fare. All thirteen of Houle's characteristics of professionalization that he suggests as appropriate content for continuing professional education could be accommodated within the ANA's guidelines.

It is especially noteworthy that Houle mentions relations to other vocations as a particularly sensitive issue among some professionalizing groups and encourages collaborative efforts at continuing education to ameliorate tensions among different, but related groups. The human resources standard of the ANA specifically addresses collaboration with other health care disciplines in meeting the identified learning needs, which suggests an openness within this group to work with others to reduce what Houle considers inevitable tensions.

It was stated earlier, but bears repeating here, that while Houle identified three modes of learning among members of professionalizing groups (instruction, inquiry, and performance), the ANA appears to focus on two (instruction and inquiry). The instruction mode is the model discussed explicitly and implicitly throughout the ANA's standards and guidelines. The ANA model of self-directed learning falls short of Houle's description of inquiry because of the former's inclusion of predetermined, behavioral objectives. Houle considers such objectives appropriate for instruction but claims that true inquiry will have outcomes that cannot be predicted. The difference between the ANA's model and Houle's is clear, but the difference does not necessarily negate the ANA model. There may be instances when self-directed learning can include predetermined objectives, as will be seen in the subsequent chapters, but the measurability of such objectives poses another problem. As indicated under persistent problems in the Introduction, some of the most significant human learning cannot be predetermined or meet a criterion of measurement. Applying aspects of the instruction mode, in this case, predetermined, behavioral objectives, to the self-directed or inquiry mode limits the range of expectations from this noninstructional mode.

Clark (1986) reports an increasing number of self-directed learning packages being used in staff development programs. More accurately, these packages should be considered "other designed" and though they may save time and money in staff development, they also may produce dependent learners, which, as Clark suggests, is counterproductive to the principles of self-directed learning.

Perhaps the greatest impediment to the ANA's efforts at promoting continuing professional education is the use of the continuing education unit (CEU) and its component, the contact hour. Whenever something as qualitative as education is converted to a quantitative mode, something is lost in the process. The artificiality of a quantity representing a quality is another persistent problem. Not that the ANA is alone in this travesty. Colleges and universities are equally guilty of forcing a qualitative entity into a quantitative one when they measure students' progress in credit hours or schedule courses into evenly divided meetings throughout a semester, trimester, or quarter. It is apparently in the interest of accountability that the CEU, like the measurable objective, is used to assure the profession and the public that responsible control is being exercised over continuing professional education.

SECTION V

A MULTIPURPOSE MODEL

By design, the Cooperative Extension Service is a multi-purpose program. It is considered the educational arm of the U.S. Department of Agriculture. From its inception in 1914 (the Smith-Lever Act) through the present it has evolved into serving four major program areas: agriculture and natural resources; home economics; 4-H youth development; and community resource development (Darkenwald and Merriam, 1982).

The program is funded by federal, state, and local units of government, hence the term "cooperative" in its title. The Smith-Lever Act formalized the relationship between the U.S. Department of Agriculture and the state land grant universities. The service is administered by the land grant universities and is committed "to the development and dissemination of practical knowledge" (Darkenwald and Merriam, p. 164).

More details of the Service's general operations will be evident in the description of the model developed by Beal and Associates (1966) contained in Chapter 9.

A Social Action Model*

T he term "curriculum" does not appear in the 510 page treatment of the Cooperative Extension Services model for planning, delivering, and evaluating educational programs for county residents (Beal et al., 1966). But, as the educational arm of the U.S. Department of Agriculture, the Service is inextricably involved in education. The program planning the authors describe can be considered synonymous with curriculum planning and the model they develop can be construed as an elaborate model of curriculum development.

The dynamic quality of the model described by Beal et al. is reflected first in the title of the book, *Social Action and Interaction in Program Planning* (1966) and in the fact that of the thirty-four separate elements in the model itself, every other one of them is an evaluation process. The continuous evaluation throughout the model contributes to the model's flexibility in accommodating different purposes. As indicated in the Introduction to this section, the Cooperative Extension Service is responsible for disseminating information and training volunteers, with regard to agricultural settings and operations, home economics, 4-H youth groups, and community resource development. The model is described in general enough terms to be applicable to all four purposes. The model is depicted in Figure 9.1.

The multipurpose curriculum model is embedded in the social ac-

---

*For a more detailed account of this model, see Beal et al. *Social Action and Interaction in Program Planning (1966).* Page references, unless otherwise indicated, are from this source.

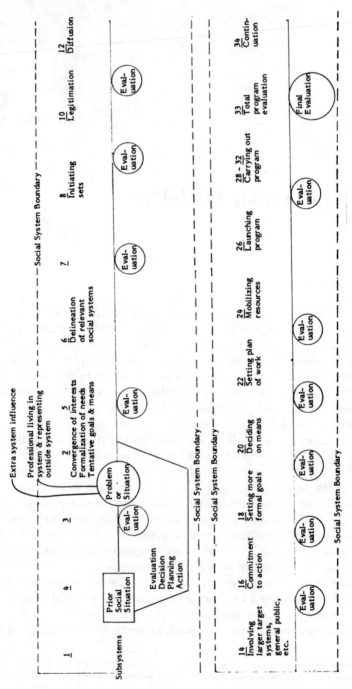

Figure 9.1   Social Action Model (adapted from Beal et al., 1966, p. 98a).

tion model described by Beal et al. (1966). Extracting the curriculum model from its context would limit the understanding of preceding actions that are necessary, according to the social action model, for the successful implementation of the curriculum. Attention then begins with the actors in the social action, the social system and its elements, and ends with a discussion of the stages of the social action model.

Actors

The success of a social action program, which, in this context includes an educational program or curriculum, is dependent upon the individuals who directly or indirectly assist in carrying it out. The specific stages within the model where selection of relevant actors is critical will be evident when the stages are described. Beal's point is that the change agent needs to be aware of how important it is to identify influential figures who can improve the chances for a program's success. He reviews a number of studies and concludes, "depending on the arena of action, the general importance of the action, and the problem area of action, different levels of influentials and different actors are involved" (p. 62). Other observations from his review include:

1. Formal office holders may or may not be influential actors.
2. Higher level influentials were seen as community problem solvers.
3. Lower level influentials were usually associated with specific problem areas (pp. 60–62).

Beal's final recommendation for change agents is to examine the steps within the model and, based on what is necessary for the next step, select resource people who have the particular skills and abilities needed for the successful completion of that next step (pp. 62–63).

Social Systems

The social systems, according to Beal et al., may be the targets for change or they may provide the resources for and be the context in which the social action occurs. Beal et al. use a conceptualization of social system developed by Loomis (1959). A social system is "a plurality of individual actors whose relations to each other are mutually oriented through the definition and mediation of a pattern of structured and shared symbols and expectations" (Loomis, 1959, p. 15, in Beal et al., 1966, p. 64).

The elements of a social system that are relevant to carrying out a social action program are:

1. End or objective—those changes which members of the social system expect to accomplish through the operation of the system.
2. Facility—the means used by the system to attain its ends.
3. Norm—the rules which prescribe what is acceptable or unacceptable.
4. Status-role—that which is to be expected from an incumbent in any social position. The two-term entity, status-role, contains the concept of status, a structural element implying position, and the concept role, a functional position.
5. Rank—the value an actor has for the system in which the rank is accorded.
6. Power—the capacity to control others. As used by Loomis there are two major forms of power, authority and influence. Authority is defined as the right, as determined by the system, to control the actions of others. Influence may be regarded as control over others which is of a nonauthoritative nature.
7. Sanctions—the rewards or penalties used to attain conformity to the ends and norms of the system.
8. Belief (knowledge)—any proposition about the universe which is thought to be true.
9. Sentiment—feelings about phenomena (p. 65).

The discussion of social systems and their elements is general in order to accommodate the wide variety of action programs and social system settings that exist. The model for social action is based on the concepts of actor and social system described above and the model's efficacy is dependent upon an understanding of the concepts and judicious use of them in planning social action programs.

Stages of the Social Action Model

Four assumptions undergird the model: 1) a complex set of interrelated functions are performed in the social action program; 2) the functions can be logically integrated to show a flow of action from beginning to end; 3) the functions can be separated into stages; and

4) methods can be devised to observe and analyze the functions at each stage (Beal et al.). In addition to these assumptions the authors offer the caveats of the model being tentative and needing further refinement. Use of the model for action or research is encouraged, but with the understanding that adjustments to specific situations may be required. Finally, the authors delineate conditions to be met for each stage of the model. These conditions can serve as evaluative devices that help to check on the translation of a conceptual stage to a pragmatic human behavior. The conditions to be met will follow the description of each stage.

Analysis of the existing social systems. The social action model is designed to work within a system as well as have an impact on a system. The latter may be referred to as a subsystem because it is contained within a larger social system. The intent at this stage is to study the elements of both the subsystem(s) and larger system. The elements, defined above, include ends, facilities, norms, status-roles, and power. Boundaries of the systems also must be analyzed. Within a county operation, the county itself may be the relevant boundary for some systems. Subsystems with the county could include government units, churches, and social organizations. Other systems may extend beyond county lines. The Red Cross and federal government agencies, for example, may be operating within a county's boundaries but, because of their broader base of operation, will be considered extracounty social systems.

The *conditions to be met* for this stage include delineation of the boundaries of the larger social system and delineation of the subsystems (groups) within the larger system. Other specific questions related to this stage are:

1. What is the relative status position of the subsystems?
2. What are the influential groups outside the system that affect it or its subsystems?
3. What are the goals and activities of the subsystems?
4. Who are the key influential leaders of the systems? (Beal et al.)

Once the context is understood, i.e., that the model is conceived as a plan for social action upon subsystems and within a larger social system, a special condition must exist in order to activate implementation of the model.

Convergence of interest. "Social action begins when the interest and definition of need of two or more people converge and the decision is made to act" (p. 76). The interests may be from people within the system or from without. The needs and goals at this stage are tentative, but sufficient to proceed to the next step.

The *conditions to be met* at this stage relate to the people whose interests converged, thus triggering possible activation of the model. Specific questions to be answered include:

1. To what extent did the people in question have adequate information about the need?
2. To what extent was there actual agreement about needs, definition of problem, and tentative goals?
3. To what extent was there agreement about the next step in the process? (Beal et al.)

These first two steps set the stage for planning with the model. The next step, evaluation, is an effort to be as thorough as possible with regard to these first two steps.

Evaluation. The conditions to be met that follow each step operate as standards by which the successful completion of the step is judged. The evaluation step encourages and reminds that each step must be completed as thoroughly as possible. Decisions regarding the planning that will follow and the "next step action" are made during evaluation. Figure 9.1 indicates an evaluation step after every other step in the model. But even this "alternating steps" approach to evaluation should not be construed as suggesting that evaluation is not a continuous process. Constant concern for evaluation of the model's steps will be evident by the conditions to be met section that follows each one.

Prior social situation. In Figure 9.1 this step appears to be out of sequence in the numbering system. Its placement in the Figure indicates some specific social situation probably preceded a convergence of interest (step 2). Attention is called to the prior situation once the convergence of interest or problem surfaces and a decision is made to proceed.

This step entails obtaining background information about the issue(s) raised in step 2. Specifically, information should be sought about past experiences with this or similar issues within the social systems. Knowledge of actors, lines of communication, cooperation, and conflicts of the past that pertain to the current issue will make subsequent planning more reliable.

The *conditions to be met* include a thorough analysis of similar activities in the past, with specific attention to the individuals or groups involved and their cooperation, conflicts, and lines of communication. Another condition is exploring the extent to which future action would have an impact on the individuals and groups. Finally, the past success and failure of an action on the issue in question (or a similar one) should be noted, and, together with the other conditions, this information should be used to help plan the strategy for the next step.

Delineation of Relevant Social Systems. The social context of the model is emphasized in this step. As stated earlier, the action plan that takes place within a social system, will likely directly affect one or more subsystems, and may need to involve systems outside the one in which the model is applied. Delineation means identifying relevant systems. Relevancy is determined by one of several criteria.

The first criterion for deciding if a social system is relevant to the planning model is determining if the members of the system will be affected by the program being planned, i.e., will the people within the system be the targets for the program? "Target systems," then, becomes a term used to denote the people (and the social system in which they operate) who will be the object of the planned actions. Other criteria for delineating systems include whether the system (and its members) will be used as resources for legitimating the action program and/or helping to carry it out.

The *conditions to be met* for this step involve identification of the target system (the one to be the object of the action), and other systems, from within and outside the social system, that may be used as resources. In addition, key individuals from these identified systems need to be delineated. Individuals should be checked regarding their representativeness of the needs and interests of the other people within their system, potential for resource to be tapped later, and representativeness regarding possible conflicting points of view.

Initiating sets. Beal et al. define the initiating set as "a group of persons (probably including the change agents previously involved) who are centrally interested in consulting with the key leaders of the relevant social systems or in some cases with the groups as a whole" (p. 80). The primary function of the initiating set is to meet with key leaders in order to obtain legitimation for the action program.

The *conditions to be met* include having confidence the members of the initiating set agreed on the role they would play in meeting with key leaders. Another condition relates to the accurate identification of key leaders from the various social systems that will be involved, i.e., were the previous two steps adequately carried out?

Legitimation with key leaders. Although final legitimation for action programs rests with the majority of people within the target system, key leaders from that system should be contacted by the initiating set to secure action or legitimation for the program. These key leaders may hold official positions within the system or may be informal leaders, who, despite not having an official position, exercise a great deal of influence within the target system.

The *conditions to be met* for this step concern the thoroughness with which the action plan was explained to the legitimizers, including problems, needs, and possible solutions. Another condition is that the legitimizers clearly understood their role in the legitimation process.

Diffusion sets. Before the diffusion sets are selected and organized, Beal et al., recommend reviewing the previous steps and considering suggestions and reactions received from key leaders in order to make major decisions about the following steps. These decisions will help to firm up what has, up to now, been a tentative plan regarding problems, needs, goals, etc.

A fairly small number of people have been involved up to this step. Success of the intended program, however, will require a larger number of people being positively disposed toward the program, before it is begun. The diffusion set should be made up of people "who can provide the kinds of resources needed (time, communication skills, organization skills, access to many people or groups, etc.) (and who will) plan activities which will give opportunities for the relevant social systems to express felt needs in relation to the problem" (p. 82). Members of the diffusion set should be able to "conceptualize and diffuse the essential ideas of the new program to the relevant target systems" (p. 83).

The *conditions to be met* are implied in the description of this step; Were decisions made about subsequent steps? Did the diffusion sets contain individuals with the requisite skills to successfully diffuse the plan? And did the members of the diffusion set agree on the goals and means they were to use?

Definition of need by the more general relevant social systems. The target system and other social systems that may be involved in assisting with the program need to be convinced that a problem exists and that there is a need for action. The diffusion sets try to accomplish this by involving members of the relevant systems in activities (ranging from surveys to demonstrations) to channel felt needs into a consensus. The objective is to make the problem the people's problem.

Beal et al. warn that this step is the most difficult and time consuming. They suggest "most of the literature available on public education and information programs leading to the securing of public actions is relevant at this stage" (p. 84).

The *conditions to be met* are the full understanding of the relevant social systems that there is a problem with which they should be concerned and that action on the problem is a high priority item for their collective agendas.

Commitment to action. Obviously, the planners have been committed to some kind of action from the beginning. The point here is to obtain commitments from members of the relevant social systems. The general rule is to receive overt, preferably public commitments.

The *conditions to be met* are obtaining overt commitments from key leaders (formal and informal) of the relevant systems.

Formulation of goals. Some goals have been at least implied from the beginning. This step involves making the goals explicit and obtaining consensus on them by the relevant social systems. The formal statement of goals could be broken into general and specific, as well as short-term, intermediate, and long-term goals. The relevant systems may simply accept the implicit goals when they are made explicit. Or the representatives or members of systems may have to formulate the goals based on their perceptions of the problems and needs. The important concern in this step is that everyone involved with the program—members of the target system and the larger system in which it exists, and those directly carrying out the program, as well as those assisting in it—be fully aware of what the goals are.

The *conditions to be met* pertain to the process by which the goals were formulated and the degree to which the goal statements are adequate and understood by the people involved.

Decision on means to be used. Once goals are decided upon, attention must be given to the means by which they will be achieved. "The type of social action programs, the social situation existing at this stage in social action, and the type of means being considered should provide some data upon which to plan the strategy for determining the range and the specificity of means and the degree and method of public involvement in determining means" (p.86). The previous three steps, from defining a need through this step on means, can be integrated. The steps are separated here for ease of description.

The *conditions to be met* deal with the adequacy of the process used to devise the means and the degree to which the means were understood by the relevant groups.

Plan of work. A specific series of actions makes up the plan of work. If a formal plan of work is written, (the authors indicate the plan of work could be informal), it should contain the following elements:

- goals to be accomplished
- means to be used
- organizational structure necessary for accomplishing the goals

- training required, if necessary, of those responsible for achieving goals
- time sequence of events (Beal et al.)

The organizational structure (number 3, above) should include lines of authority and a clear description of which people or groups are responsible for which actions.

The *conditions to be met* for the plan of work include the degree to which each of the five elements is adequately described.

Mobilizing resources. Human, physical, and financial resources necessary to carry out the plan of work should be fully mobilized at this step. Implicit in the mobilization is the need to organize resources to assure achievement of the goals.

The *conditions to be met* include the extent to which all resources called for in the plan of work were mobilized. In addition, the organizational structure should have been explained to and understood by all those who would be involved in the plan of action.

Action steps. The number of action steps depends on the plan of work. Assuming a single purpose for the overall action plan, the plan of work would guide the number and kind of action steps necessary to meet the goals. But the model is robust enough to accommodate more than one purpose at a time, in which case "action steps" could be the beginning of a new plan, starting with "convergence of interest."

The *condition to be met*, assuming a one purpose use of the model, is simply the adequacy of carrying out each of the action steps.

Total program evaluation. Placement of this step at the end of the model should not suggest evaluation is to be thought of only as a terminal step. Each of the previous steps has been followed with a section called "conditions to be met," which operated as a formative evaluation—a check on each process step as the model was applied.

The total program evaluation is the step at which progress toward goals is assessed. It also includes attention to the means by which the goals were sought and the adequacy of the organizational structure in carrying out the plan of work. This summative evaluation should provide insights for future use of the model.

The *conditions to be met* include the adequacy of the periodic evaluations throughout the model and the degree to which the final evaluation assessed the overall impact of using the model as a guide to social action.

Continuation. The final evaluation may yield information that suggests continuing with action steps in order to achieve more completely the goals of the plan of work. The continued efforts usually apply only to the long-range goals, but the intermediate and short-term goals may require a continuation of action steps as well.

Commentary

The model for social action is general enough to accommodate different purposes, hence its classification as multipurpose. The model was developed by sociologists interested in and experienced with the Cooperative Extension Service, a multipurpose enterprise in itself.

The model assumes a change-agent working within a social system context. The actors of the system, the various subsystems, and the steps or stages of the model are described at a general enough level to permit application to a variety of specific situations.

The placement of an evaluation process after every step encourages reflective action throughout the model. Adjustments to the model might have to be made in any specific application if the process evaluations revealed less than adequate performance of any of the steps.

The successful use of the model clearly requires identification and use of key leaders within the social system. In some situations it appears as if the model may carry seeds of its own destruction. Successful use of the model is based on securing legitimation from key leaders within the system. If the plan of action threatened a leader's status within the system, it would appear the plan would be doomed. The model, in this regard, may be seen as one that basically supports the system in which it works and may not be capable of effecting any change that would significantly affect the status of formal and informal leaders.

SECTION VI

SELF-DIRECTED
LEARNING

Curriculum models usually have an institutional base. And within an institution, creating access to knowledge is conventionally conceived as a top-down process, i.e., an educator creates access for learners. Brookfield (1986) and Joyce (1971) effectively argue that the tie to an institution is oftentimes a limiting factor in designing educational experiences. But adult education, unlike conventional, K-12 schooling, need not be institution-bound. Therefore, creating access to knowledge, likewise, need not be an act performed *for* someone else. Adults can and do direct their own learning. A self-directed learner is more likely to gain access to knowledge, as opposed to having someone else create the access. It has only recently been studied, beginning in the 1960s, but self-directed learning appears to be part of a new conception of person; one who is viewed as "a self-directing organism with initiative, intentions, choices, freedom, energy, and responsibility" (Tough, 1979, p. 5).

Two pioneer thinkers in the field of self-directed learning are Allen Tough and Malcolm Knowles. Their descriptions and discussions of the various aspects of self-directed learning constitute this section. Citing their work within the context of curriculum models will provide curriculum developers the learner's perspective. The descriptions may be more important than all of the other models, because self-directed learning is more common than all of the acquired learning through the other curriculum models combined.

The emphasis in the works of Tough and Knowles is on the management of education—the gaining access phase—and not really on learning per se. The descriptions, therefore, will be on the managing and controlling of resources without specific regard for either full awareness of alternatives or challenge and recreation of personally held beliefs and constructs (Brookfield, 1986).

CHAPTER 10

Tough's Description
of Self-Directed Learning*

Tough conducted a number of studies of self-directed learning in the 1960s and 1970s. Several other researchers carried out similar studies and their findings, supplementing his own, are used as the base for his generalizations about self-directed learning. The emphasis here will be on Tough's treatment of what is learned, reasons for learning, and then decisions related to planning to learn, and seeking and obtaining help in learning. Figure 10.1 depicts the essential elements in self-directed learning. Some definitions are necessary, however, before examining the various elements of self-directed learning.

Episodes and learning projects.

An episode is "a well-defined period of time that is held together by the similarity in intent, activity, or place of the thoughts and actions that occur during it" (p. 8). Tough further suggests that episodes are not interrupted for more than two or three minutes and can last for thirty to sixty minutes, some being shorter and some lasting longer. The episode is a basic unit or "chunk" of time Tough found people

---

*For a more detailed account of Tough's work, see Tough, A. *The Adult's Learning Projects: A Fresh Approach to Theory and Practice in Adult Learning* (1979). Unless otherwise indicated all references in this chapter will be to this source.

using rather naturally in describing the various ways in which they learned on their own. The episode then, is the building block of larger activities, but before an episode can be considered a part of a learning project, it must meet four other criteria.

Intention to learn. A very deliberate learning episode, Tough maintains, must reveal an intention to gain certain knowledge and skill. The term knowledge and skill includes:

> . . . any positive desired changes or improvement in a person's knowledge, awareness, comprehension, beliefs, ability to apply, ability to analyze and synthesize, ability to evaluate, judgment, perceptual skills, physical skills, competence or performance, response tendencies, habits, attitudes, emotional reactions, recall, sensitivity, insight, confidence, patience and self-control, and/or some other personality characteristic, inner behavior, or overt behavior (p. 9).

The changes that qualify are those that result "from what a person sees, hears, feels, thinks, or does" (p. 9).

Specificity of intent. Another criterion Tough applies is that the knowledge and skill a person seeks is fairly clear and definite in that person's mind before the episode begins. This criterion rules out of consideration learning experiences that might occur as a result of attending a museum or exposition, taking a trip, or changing jobs. Only when the person has a fairly clear and definite expectation of the knowledge and skill to be learned is it considered a learning episode.

Retention. The third criterion Tough considers is the intention that the knowledge and skill will be retained for a minimum of two days. Tough admits this is an arbitrary designation, but one that has to be made if clear understanding is to be achieved when conducting interviews to determine the amount of self-directed learning a person experiences, as well as communicating the results. The retention criterion would exclude learning efforts undertaken for such short-term reasons as assembling a toy or purchasing an appliance; efforts not likely to result in retaining knowledge or skill beyond the two day minimum.

Priority of learning intention. The last criterion applied to an episode is that of major intention. If a person's motivation to gain and retain certain knowledge and skill accounts for more than 50 percent of the reasons for learning, it is considered a deliberate learning episode. Learning can and does occur serendipitously, but Tough has chosen to focus only on those episodes where more than half a person's

.____Overview

.____Definitions

.____Frequency

.____Purposes for learning

.____What is learned   .____Why learning occurs
.____Six categories   .____Six reasons

.____Deciding to begin

.____Preparatory steps   .____Assistance

.____Choosing a planner

.____Self as planner

.____Group or leader

.____One-to-one

.____Nonhuman resource

.____Advantages and disadvantages

Figure 10.1 *Outline of Essential Elements in Self-Directed Learning (Adapted from Tough, 1979).*

intention is to learn. Tough explains the use of this criterion by alluding to the role of helper:

> The adult's highly deliberate efforts to learn provide an excellent starting point for developing a better competence and help in adult learning. A person may be willing to accept help (and accept opportunities for developing his own competence) with something he is *trying* to accomplish. He is not so likely to accept help with something for which his motivation is low (p. 13. Emphasis in the original).

Tough further claims the intention criterion does not rule out a majority of learning episodes and, until his and others' efforts were applied, the phenomenon of intentional self-directed learning had received scant attention by researchers.

Once a learning episode is understood to mean one that satisfies the four criteria, Tough defines a learning project as "a series of clearly related episodes" (p. 14). Self-directed learning revolves around learning projects that are made up of related learning episodes. The nature of the episodes within a project can take many forms, e.g., reading a book, listening to a lecture, etc., but they are related in the sense that they all contribute to gaining knowledge and skill associated with a learning project.

The final operational definition involves the use of time as a criterion applied to a learning project. Tough uses a minimum of seven hours for a project that has taken place in the last six month period. Projects of shorter duration or spread over more than six months are judged by Tough as minor efforts that are neither significant nor intensive.

What people learn.

A wide range of knowledge and skill constitutes the content of adults' learning projects. Tough discusses six categories of content that serve different purposes for the learners. His discussions of why learning projects are undertaken are separate from his discussions of content, although the six content categories revolve around six somewhat different purposes for learning.

The first category is "preparing for an occupation, and then keeping up" (p. 35). This category includes learning projects that involve getting ready for a new job or maintaining or improving competence on a current job. Related to this general occupational category is the second category that includes specific job-related learning projects that tend to be more focused than the projects in the first category. Tough calls this second category "specific tasks and problems on the job" (p. 36).

A third category is "learning for home and personal responsibilities" (p. 37). Learning about sewing, cooking, home repair, or maintenance represents many of the projects included in this category. In addition, learning projects involving improvement in such endeavors as child rearing, family finance, and home purchases are included in this category.

A fourth category is called "improving some broad area of competence" (p. 38). Efforts directed toward obtaining a better understanding of groups and individuals, or such phenomena as leadership and followership, or other efforts to improve one's interpersonal relations are included in this category. Seeking improvement in writing ability and public speaking, and learning more about dieting and physical exercise also fall within this fourth category.

"Learning for interest or leisure" (p. 38) is the fifth category established by Tough. Hobbies and other leisure time activities account for the learning in this category. The sixth and final category is "curiosity or a question about certain subject matter" (p. 39). Studying geography through travel or reading because one is simply interested in learning more about an area or region, are examples of a learning project in this category. Learning more about a particular religion is another example.

Except for learning projects in the last category (simple curiosity or question), Tough claims "some anticipated use or application of the knowledge and skill is the strongest motivation for the majority of learning projects" (p. 39). Citing a number of studies carried out in other countries, as well as theoretical statements from other writers in the field, Tough underscores the importance of utility to people when deciding to carry out a learning project.

Why people learn.

As pointed out earlier, the content categories Tough derived from his research permit some inferences about why people learn. Tough's approach to the question of why is more pointed, however, in that he is probing the person's perceived benefit to be enjoyed as a result of the learning project. A person might carry out a learning project related to an occupation (category 1), but expect to benefit in terms of a promotion or raise in salary. The two purposes (improving competence and increasing the likelihood of a promotion) are not incompatible. The former is considered by Tough as a category for the content and the latter as motivation for action.

A person's motivation for carrying out a learning project usually concerns an intention to use the knowledge and skill. Tough claims the anticipation to use or apply what will be learned

> . . . is the strongest reason in the majority of adult learning projects
> . . . (and) even when it is not the strongest reason, the intention of using or applying the knowledge and skill is often present to some extent in a learning project (p. 50).

This concern for utility typically limits the amount of learning, i.e., once enough is learned to be useful for the problem at hand, the learning project will be discontinued. If and when new knowledge or skill is required, the learner will resume the learning project.

Utility alone, however, does not account entirely for reasons why a person undertakes a learning project. Tough claims a desire to do a better job (because of learning certain knowledge and skill) often is cited as a reason for learning. In other words, the responsibility for a job could be fulfilled without the learning, but the learning contributes to doing the job well. This sense of satisfaction is felt during the application of the recently acquired knowledge and skill and may continue as a motivation even after a job is performed. Satisfaction also may be realized if the learner is able to perform the job more efficiently than before. By investing time in learning, the individual will be able to save time in work.

Another motivating factor for engaging in a learning project may be the need to impart the knowledge or skill. The responsibility for giving a speech, writing a report, or presenting a lesson or demonstration may trigger the need to initiate and carry out a learning project.

Learning for future understanding is a third motivation that differs somewhat from the first two. Applying the knowledge and skill to a problem or presenting them to others concern producing or imparting; whereas learning for future understanding involves taking in knowledge and skill. Aquiring a special vocabulary before studying more about a subject is an example of learning that is done with future learning in mind.

Simply possessing knowledge, without actually applying it, may provide pleasure and self-esteem that can serve as motivation for learning. The positive feelings of joy and happiness can accrue to individuals who learn some knowledge and skill. Tough reports these feelings alone can account for why some people embark on a learning project. Self-esteem, likewise, may be the primary motive for learning. A person may feel capable of becoming a better spouse, parent, or Christian by possessing certain knowledge and skill.

Learning for credit is another motivation Tough discovered learners have for undertaking a learning project. The newly acquired knowledge and skill may be necessary to pass an examination successfully, e.g., learning rules for driving an automobile to pass a driver's test. Or the knowledge and skill may not actually be applied, but inferred by others because of certain processes, such as attending a class or passing a written test.

Finally, Tough reports there are immediate benefits a person expects from gaining some knowledge and skill. These benefits are not necessarily related to application, but come instead actually during the learning project. Tough describes seven such benefits:

1. Satisfying curiosity, puzzlement, or a question
2. Enjoyment from the content itself
3. Enjoyment from practicing the skill
4. The activity of learning
5. Learning successfully
6. Completing unfinished learning
7. Aspects unrelated to learning (e.g., the social, escapist, or breaking from the routine) (pp. 59–62).

The intention to use the knowledge and skill derived from a learning project is considered by Tough as the most common and powerful motivation for an adult's self-directed learning. But other reasons exist as well and determining their relative importance is one of the challenges remaining for those who wish to contribute to the continuing study of why adults learn.

Deciding to begin.

Attention now turns to the steps that are necessary for a learner in deciding whether to begin a learning project, determining what knowledge and skill need to be learned, and seeking help in carrying out the project. Tough has found up to sixty conceptually distinct steps that could be taken by a learner when anticipating a learning project. Not all learners take that many steps, but the possibilities, if not overwhelming, certainly underscore the contention that deciding to learn can be a complex process. An excerpt from one of Tough's accounts captures the myriad aspects of deciding to learn:

> He tentatively or definitely adopts, modifies, or drops some action goal (or some desired level for an action goal). Or he assesses the strength of his desire for achieving that action goal or level . . . As part of this step, the person may perform several other detailed steps. Perhaps, for example, he (a) sets long-term life goals or career goals, or examines his philosophy of life or his basic values; (b) estimates the probable benefits from some action goal or level; (c) estimates the present or future needs or problems of some organization or of society . . . (p. 66).

Despite the complexity of considerations in making the decision to begin a learning project, Tough reports most adults begin with little or no help. He indicates, however, that many times an adult would prefer more help in making the decision to begin.

The appropriateness of the help received in deciding whether and what to learn revolves around influence on and control of the learner. Tough lists seven ideal characteristics of helpers that illustrate what he considers appropriate help.

1. None of the helper's influence results from providing inaccurate or unrealistic information.
2. None of his influence is harmful.
3. Most of the influence is sought by the learner, or at least eventually welcomed by him.
4. The helper does not try to produce much more influence than he actually succeeds in producing, and his concern for what or how much is learned is not greater than the learner's concern.
5. The help is designed for the particular learner.
6. Any influence exerted by the helper results from the learner's trust in his judgement, or from the helper's contagious enthusiasm, not from his control over certain future rewards or other consequences for the learner.
7. As a result of his interaction with the helper, the person develops a stronger tendency to learn in the future whenever he becomes aware of some problem, responsibility, or significant subject matter (pp. 73–74).

The ideal characteristics of a helper could be refined, Tough believes, if programs were offered that assisted learners with setting goals for learning.

Choosing a planner.

A planner is defined by Tough as:

> . . . the person (or group or object) that does most of the day-to-day planning in the learning project . . . the planner makes the majority of the decisions about what to learn (the detailed knowledge and skill) in each learning episode, and/or about how to learn (the detailed strategy, activities, and resources) (p. 77).

Tough classifies four types of planners: self; a group or leader of a group; a one-to-one helper; and a nonhuman resource. The frequency of choice is roughly; one's self (about 73%); a group or leader of a group (about 14%); a one-to-one helper (about 10%); and a nonhuman resource (about 3%) (p. 173).

The choice of one's self as planner has several advantages. Tough describes eleven advantages that can be summarized as interest in control and autonomy concerning various aspects of the learning project. The learner, for example, may believe time would be lost if someone else planned the project; or that a planner's help would not satisfy the learner's needs or match a preferred style of learning.

Choosing one's self as the planner does not preclude enlisting the help of others in carrying out a learning project. Advice, encouragement, and information are frequently received by learners from friends, colleagues, family members, and others, but, as Tough emphasizes, these helpers "do not *control* the learning project" (p. 99. Emphasis in the original).

Seeking help when one is a self-planner typically involves the following steps:

The learner:
- develops a general awareness of the need for help;
- becomes fairly specific about what is needed;
- selects a particular resource, perhaps after seeking advice about this decision;
- decides how to approach the individual or obtain the resource;
- takes that action (p. 99).

Tough advises, however, that obtaining help is not always as rational as the steps would imply. Individuals frequently act on impulse or by accident may discover a resource. A significant finding Tough reports is from a doctoral study that indicated the least important reasons for choosing a particular helper were expertise, education, and relevant experience, in contrast to the most important reasons of feeling comfortable, relaxed, and able to talk freely with the helper.

Self-planned learning is seldom, if ever, carried out in a vacuum. Tough reports helpers number between five and twenty typically. They may be friends or neighbors or members of the family. Many times helpers are professionals whose responsibilities include providing such help. They may be medical doctors, pharmacists, or attorneys. Nearly every adult, besides being a learner, may also be an appropriate helper to another learner.

Nonhuman resources frequently serve as helpers. Placed within this category are all printed materials, television, radio, exhibits, and computers, to name a few. It would be unlikely that a self-planned learning project could be conducted without a wide array of human and nonhuman resources.

The advantages associated with using one's self as the planner are the feelings of autonomy and control that accrue and are reinforced as the learner proceeds through a project. Assuming the learners are competent in all the preparatory steps necessary for a learning project, they can celebrate the exhiliration associated with being masters of their "fate." But the assumption is just that. Tough suggests a number of difficulties typically encountered during the planning stage that self-helpers experience.

The disadvantages to helping one's self are the time, energy, and sometimes money, wasted when the learner is not sufficiently competent in deciding exactly what to learn and the appropriate activities, materials, and resources necessary for learning. The ability to deal effectively with logistical problems—where and when to learn—as well as maintaining motivation to learn, are additional barriers the self-planner needs to overcome. Failure in any of the preparatory steps will result not only in incomplete learning, but more important, in a decrease in confidence to mount other learning projects.

A self-directed learner can use a group or its leader to make most of the decisions about what should be learned and in what manner. The leader of the group could be a volunteer who emerges by consensus, or is appointed. The leader may be a professional in the field with much experience in leading groups and individuals, or an amateur with little or no experience as a leader in helping others learn.

Tough describes a variety of group formats, including autonomous learning groups, that, by definition, are without a designated leader or affiliation. The groups are "of equals" and responsibility for planning content and activities is shared among members. He estimates about 20 percent of all group-directed projects are of this type.

The advantages of using a group or its leader as a planner for learning projects are several. The overriding concern, however, applies equally to the disadvantage side of the coin: the degree to which the group and/or its leader meet the needs of the learner. Use of a group can result in new associations, increased motivation, and a measure of anonymity that may be desired. The disadvantages include scheduling, time and expense of travel to and from a group, and lack of individual attention to unique needs and interests.

Using a person in a one-to-one relationship as a planning resource has been cited as the most efficient way to learn. (Bloom, 1981). Common examples are learning to drive a car, improving athletic performance, and learning to play a musical instrument. In a one-to-one relationship the planner makes the decisions about what to learn and how best to learn it. The planner may spend a lot of time diagnosing specific learning needs or simply prescribe activities with little regard for the learner's uniqueness.

The advantages of a one-to-one planning relationship include the learner receiving the undivided attention of the planner, which maximizes oportunities for questions and answers and other immediate feedback that the learner can use to adjust learning efforts appropriately. The planner may be able to provide the actual subject matter or other resources necessary for completing a learning project. Overall the sheer convenience, some would say luxury, of having an expert direct the learning experiences of an amateur appear to outweigh any disadvantages. Nonetheless, as Tough notes, the one-to-one relationship is used quite infrequently by learners. He speculates that cost may appear to be prohibitive, but that even when free, "the learner may be reluctant to consume so many hours of the other person's time" (p. 132).

Finally, a nonhuman resource may serve as a planner. Obviously, books and other printed materials, audio tapes, computer programs, and other "nonhuman" resources have a human origin. Somebody planned or wrote them with some kind of potential learner in mind. Whatever the format, the learner decides to let the nonhuman resource determine the day-to-day strategies in aquiring the knowledge and skill being pursued.

Programmed materials provide some accommodation for different levels of ability by branching patterns that enable a learner to satisfy some prerequisite learning before proceeding with the main objective(s). Feedback is provided for reinforcement and built-in tests assure a minimum level of confidence. Computer-based instruction and interactive video, wherein a learner interacts with a computer-based program, may involve more sophisticated forms of programming.

The chief advantage of nonhuman resources is that they usually represent the efforts of expert talent in subject matter and technology. A television documentary, for example, may combine the expertise of a number of authorities who otherwise would not be assembled. Tough notes that printed materials, recordings, or television programs may be "the quickest route for gaining certain types of knowledge and skill, such as a technical skill or cognitive subject matter that is detailed (step-by-step), specific, and clearly defined" (p. 127). Examples of such areas of interest are acquiring physical fitness and learning a foreign language.

Other advantages of nonhuman resources are that they will not intimidate, humiliate, or become impatient. A learner can modify instructions or abandon them altogether without fear of embarrassment. The primary disadvantage is their very same impersonal characteristic, i.e., they do not respond as another human in terms of companionship or interaction which many learners want.

Tough concludes his discussion of self-directed learning projects by suggesting some implications for instructors and institutions. Those implications relate well to the commentary below.

Commentary

As was pointed out at the beginning of this section, curriculum models portray how access to knowledge can be created. The perspective is typically from the top down. The area of self-directed learning, however, provides the learner's perspective as one of gaining access, which is more of a bottom to top orientation.

The implications for the curriculum director revolve around facilitating the management and control of educational resources that will enable the learner to become more efficient at learning. Specific areas of setting learning goals, obtaining resources, and evaluating progress could become skill courses offered to learners. The very subject of self-directed learning itself could be a general area about which courses and seminars could be developed. Curriculum models in adult education need not be mutually exclusive of models of self-directed learning. Indeed, curriculum development personnel should use both to achieve a blend of efforts that help people become more proficient as self-directed learners.

CHAPTER 11

Knowles' Self-Directed Learning*

U nlike Tough's model of self-directed learning, which was an out-growth of his research of the phenomenon and consequently was essentially descriptive in nature, Knowles' model is primarily pre-scriptive. Indeed, his text is cast as a source book, as the subtitle in-dicates, to help learners and teachers better plan for self-directed learning. As was the case regarding Tough's model, it is more accurate to consider the model appropriate for self-directed education, because the emphasis is on managing resources for learning.

Figure 11.1 contains the elements of the self-directed learning model Knowles discusses. His model includes self-directed learners' needs as well as the needs of facilitators or teachers interested in promoting self-directed learning in their students.

Definitions

Although many labels have been used to describe self-directed learning, Knowles defines it as,

a process in which individuals take the initiative, with or without the help of others, in diagnosing their learning needs, formulating learning goals,

---

*For a more detailed description of this model, see Knowles, M.S. *Self Directed Learning: A Guide for Learners and Teachers* (1975). Unless otherwise indicated, all references in this chapter will be to this source.

identifying human and material resources for learning, choosing and implementing appropriate learning strategies, and evaluating learning outcomes (p. 18).

Such terms as self-planned learning, self-teaching, and autonomous learning Knowles notes have been used to mean the same as self-directed learning, but he prefers not to use them because they imply learning in isolation. He asserts "self-directed learning usually takes place in association with various kinds of helpers, such as teachers, tutors, mentors, resource people, and peers" (p. 18). The opposite of

Self-Directed Learning

Definitions
Rationale
Assumptions
Processes

Facilitator/Teacher   Learner

A new role   Self-concept

Competencies   Competencies

- Setting an appropriate climate   - Relationship with others

- Planning   - Self-assessment

- Diagnosising needs   - Translating learning needs

- Setting goals   into objectives

- Designing a learning plan   - Selecting effective

- Engaging in learning activities   strategies

- Consulting   - Collecting and evaluating

- Evaluating learning outcomes   evidence of accomplishment

Developing a learning contract

Figure 11.1   *Knowles' Model of Self-Directed Learning (Knowles, 1975)*

self-directed learning is teacher-directed learning, and by exploring the different assumptions upon which each is built, the rationale for understanding self-directed learning will be addressed.

Rationale

Knowles cites several reasons why self-directed learning should be receiving more attention than the conventional teacher-directed learning. More effective learning occurs, he claims, when learners take the initiative. Longer retention and more use is made of the learning when learners are motivated by their own purposes rather than by external sources.

Knowles also sees self-directed learning as part of a natural progression from the dependency of childhood to independence in adulthood. He claims "an essential aspect of maturing is developing the ability to take increasing responsibility for our own lives—to become increasingly self-directing" (p. 15).

A third reason for nurturing self-directed learning is the advent of new programs that require learner initiative for successful completion. Individual study programs, external degrees, and universities-without-walls all place more emphasis on learners being able to take the initiative and assume responsibility regarding their own learning.

A fourth reason for addressing self-directed learning is related to the rapidly changing world in which we live. If conventional, teacher-directed learning involves almost exclusively the transmission of knowledge, then the effectiveness of that model will be adversely affected by the increased rate of change occurring now and in the future. Unlike a hundred years ago, the stability of the knowledge base in so many fields of study has been disrupted by new discoveries and technologies that appear at an increasing rate. Looking ahead, Knowles predicts, "rapid change will be the only stable characteristic" (p. 15). Survival under such conditions will be enhanced if learners develop skills of inquiry to permit continuous learning throughout a lifetime.

An extension of the lifelong learning idea is that a reconception of learning from "being taught" to capitalizing on life experiences as learning experiences is necessary. Replacing the notion that learning has to be associated with an educational institution with the realization that learning can and does take place all the time in and out of organizations and with and without other people is another necessity if self-directed learning is to receive the kind of attention it deserves.

Assumptions

Knowles contrasts self-directed learning with learning that is teacher-directed, the latter being typically associated with conventional K-12 schooling and referred to in the literature as pedagogy. He suggests andragogy, "the art and science of helping adults (or even better, maturing human beings) learn" (p. 60) is a more apt term for self-directed learning because it is built upon assumptions that are significantly different from the assumptions associated with pedagogy. A summary of Knowles' comparison of the assumptions appears below.

Concept of the learner. Teacher-directed procedures generally assume a dependent personality, whereas when self-directed activities are encouraged an increasingly self-directed individual is assumed.

Role of learner's experience. Pedagogical practices assume the learner's experience is to be built upon, rather than be used as a resource. Andragogical efforts consider the learner's experience as a rich resource for further learning.

Readiness to learn. Teacher-directed learning is based upon the assumption that readiness varies with levels of maturation. Self-directed learning assumes readiness develops from life tasks and problems of the learner.

Orientation to learning. The emphasis for teacher-directed activities typically is on subject matter, whereas self-directed learning usually revolves around a task or problem.

Motivation. Pedagogy is often based on external rewards and punishments. Andragogy assumes internal incentives, such as curiosity, will motivate the learner.

Knowles cautions that the interpretations of the differences between pedagogy (teacher-directed) and andragogy (self-directed) should be viewed as variations on a spectrum, not seen as "black and white differences" (p. 60). He further contrasts the two in terms of process or procedure followed by each.

Processes

Each of the assumptions described above includes implications for corresponding processes. Knowles' comparisons below warrant the same caution as the assumptions, i.e., they reflect emphases and are not necessarily mutually exclusive.

Climate. Adjectives associated with the climate of teacher-directed learning activities include: "formal; authority-oriented; competitive;

and judgmental" (p. 60). Self-directed activities flourish when the climate is "informal, mutually respectful, consensual, collaborative, and supportive" (p. 60).

Planning. Pedagogical practices rely on the teacher doing the majority of the planning. Andragogy includes shared decision-making as the primary mode of planning.

Diagnosis of needs. Teacher-directed learning prescribes activities based upon the teacher's diagnosis of needs. Self-directed learning evolves from a mutual assessment of needs.

Setting goals. Teachers set the goals in teacher-directed learning activities, whereas the goals are mutually negotiated in a self-directed situation.

Designing a learning plan. The plan is designed by the teacher in a pedagogical setting and can be characterized as having a subject matter focus and a logical sequence. Andragogical learning plans frequently include learning contracts and a sequence based on readiness to learn.

Learning activities. Teacher-directed learning usually involves transmitting knowledge. Didactic teaching, for example, includes telling or assigning readings for the learner to acquire information. Self-directed learning emphasizes an inquiry approach, including independent projects and capitalizing on experiential learning.

Evaluation. Pedagogy utilizes teacher evalution in an external, reward or punishment mode, whereas andragogy entails a mutual assessment by teacher and student.

Self-Concept

Knowles addresses the self-concept of the self-directed learner by including passages from the professional literature that speak to the ideal of being a self-directed person. No single description of an idealized self captures the myriad aspects. By including selections from a variety of writers, Knowles intends to "help you construct a model for yourself and, by comparing where you are now in your thinking about yourself with that model, discover aspects of your self-concept that might need strengthening" (p. 64).

Competencies

Learners who want to improve their self-directed learning effectiveness and teachers or facilitators who wish to promote self-directed learning should have certain competencies. A shared competency that both learners and teachers need, according to Knowles, is the ability to explain to others the different assumptions and skills associated with teacher-directed learning and self-directed learning. Beyond this understanding, the competencies for learners and facilitators are somewhat different. The learner's competencies will be described first, followed by competencies necessary for the facilitation of self-directed learning.

Relationships with others. Knowles asserts, "self-directed learning can flourish only when learners and teachers see one another as mutually helpful human beings with resources to share" (p. 71). Conventional, teacher-directed experiences tend to cast learners into an environment that encourages them to consider the teacher as the authority and fellow learners as competitors. Self-directed learning requires more collaboration and comradeship. Knowles offers an activity designed to enhance relationship-building (pp. 71–74).

Self-assessment. The beginning of a self-directed learning project includes becoming aware of a need for learning. Planning a learning experience will be much easier if the learner is clear about the particular learning needs. Knowles suggests three steps to self-assessment:

1. The development of a model of desired behaviors or required competencies;
2. the assessment of the present level of performance by the individual in each of these behaviors or competencies; and
3. the assessment of the gaps between the model and the present performance (pp. 81–82).

Developing a model of competency involves learning what knowledge, skill, or attitudes are associated with competent performance in the area under question. Knowles discusses four sources that can be used in learning about ideal models: research, judgment of experts, task analysis, and group participation. Each source has advantages and disadvantages regarding its usefulness to self-directed learners. The overriding concern is that learners understand the source well enough to restate the model in their own terms, thereby making the model more of a personal construction as opposed to something entirely external and perceived as being imposed.

The second step in self-assessment involves assessing one's present level of performance. Knowles cautions:

We are not talking here about a highly precise mathematical process of quantitative measurement of the full range of behaviors for performing any set of functions . . . Rather, we are talking about a process that is more sensitizing than measuring, more concerned with setting broad directions of growth rather than defining terminal behaviors (p. 86).

Knowles believes too little is known about human behavior to be able to be very much more precise regarding assessment. His prognosis, based on the complexity of human nature, is that achieving such precision in assessment may well be unrealistic.

The actual assessment then is a comparison of one's present level of knowledge or performance with that of the model. Whether a learner actually takes a pencil and paper test to assess knowledge or has performance reviewed by another person, the final assessment involves matching one's own knowledge or performance with the model's and identifying the areas that do not measure up.

Translating learning needs into objectives. The actual form an objective takes is less important than the criterion of clarity. Knowles uses five categories for objectives. The use of categories makes it easier to select learning strategies because certain strategies are more appropriate for achieving certain types of objectives than others. Knowles' categories are:

- To develop knowledge about . . .
- To develop understanding of . . .
- To develop skill in . . .
- To develop attitudes toward . . .
- To develop values of . . .(p. 98).

Knowles considers his treatment of objectives as being "in the broad humanistic sense of self-determined directions of self-development, with the instructor and the students participating mutually in the process of their formulation" (p. 96). The specificity of performance objectives commonly associated with training is not considered appropriate for this broad humanistic approach.

Selecting effective strategies. As was indicated above, certain educational strategies are more appropriate than others for certain types of objectives. Not that there is a perfect one-to-one correspondence between method and goal, but some methods are more frequently indicated for some goals than are others. Knowles suggests a number of methods for each of his five types of objectives. Excerpts from his presentation (p. 104) appear below.

1. Knowledge—	Lecture, debate, interview, motion picture, reading, programmed instruction.
2. Understanding—	Audience participation, demonstration, dramatization, Socratic discussion, case method, and simulation games.
3. Skills—	Skill practice exercises, role-playing, drill, and coaching.
4. Attitudes—	Experience-sharing discussion, sensitivity training, role-playing, critical incident process, case method, and group therapy.
5. Values—	Value-clarification exercises, biographical reading, lecture, debate, symposium, and role-playing.

Self-directed learners should be familiar enough with various methods to choose judiciously among them, depending on the kinds of objectives they want to achieve.

Collecting and evaluating evidence of accomplishment. Just as certain strategies are appropriate for certain objectives, different kinds of evaluative evidence are likewise more appropriate than others, depending on the objective being assessed. Using the same five categories of objectives used for selecting methods for learning, Knowles suggests corresponding evaluative procedures (pp. 110–111).

1. Knowledge—	"Reports of knowledge acquired, as in essays, examinations, oral presentations, audiovisual presentations" (p. 110).
2. Understanding—	Being able to use knowledge in solving problems or in simulation games. Planning projects to learn more about a knowledge area.
3. Skills—	Actual performance that may be rated by others.
4. Attitudes—	Attitude inventory score. Actual performance in role playing that is rated by others.
5. Values—	Performance in value clarification group or in simulation games with feedback from others.

Information from the evaluations can be used to decide how well the objectives have been achieved. If gaps still exist, for example, between current level of performance and that of an ideal model, the learner could again begin the process of setting objectives, selecting strategies, etc. until objectives are satisfactorily accomplished.

Facilitator/Teacher

Knowles addresses the requirements for teachers who wish to promote self-directed learning among the students in their charge. He discusses eight competencies teachers should have if they hope to be successful in helping students become more self-directed. All eight competencies evolve out of the new role of the teacher—that of facilitator of learning.

A new role. The conventional role of teacher is that of transmitter of content. Knowles sees four major responsibilities associated with the conventional role. Stated as questions these responsibilities include:

1. What content needs to be covered?
2. How can this content be organized into manageable units?
3. How can these units be organized into a logical sequence?
4. What means of transmission will be most efficient for transmitting each unit (pp. 31–32)?

Some kind of evaluation would be planned, in addition to the content transmission plans, in order to assess how well the students learned the content.

The conventional teacher acted in a one-way channel—from the top down to the students. The new role, facilitator of learning, requires more collaboration with students and supports a two-way channel of communication. The facilitator role requires a change from content transmission to one that is concerned with content acquisition. The emphasis in the new role is on the process of helping (facilitating) the learner to acquire the knowledge and skills chosen. Knowles discusses the competencies required of this new role.

Competencies of the Facilitator

The areas in which the facilitator should develop competencies roughly correspond to the competencies self-directed learners should have so they may become more independent as learners. The first concern, according to Knowles, is the climate in which learning will take place.

Setting an appropriate climate. Attention to the climate or setting begins with having the learners get to know one another and relating to one another in a collaborative rather than competitive manner. Informing the learners that instead of the conventional, teacher-directed setting, all too familiar for most students, the current one will involve a facilitator role, wherein the "teacher" will act as a process consultant and resource for content. The process emphasis will mark the shift from transmitting content to helping learners plan and carry out their self-directed learning. Knowles suggests a climate "characterized by both mutual caring and support and intellectual rigor" (p. 35).

Planning. The facilitator must plan, but also must realize the built-in contradiction of planning for self-directed learning. The planning, therefore, is bounded by process concerns—deciding on procedures or deciding who should decide on procedures. Depending on the size of the group, the facilitator must consider the kind and amount of group decision making that will be feasible. For example, with a large group, a representative steering committee might decide on procedures and with a group smaller than thirty, all the learners may vote. Plans, or more appropriately, contingency plans, should be thought through before meeting with the learners.

Diagnosing needs for learning. The challenge to the facilitator in helping learners diagnose their needs is to use a model of competencies with which the learners can identify. If the facilitator prepares a model, the risk is that the learners will perceive it as something simply imposed on them. Knowles suggests learners be given an opportunity to at least modify an already developed model or actually construct their own ideal to insure their having a sense of ownership in the finally agreed upon model. Once a model representing the competencies is established, the facilitator must make it possible for learners to assess their present levels of development, vis á vis the ideal model, in order to discover their learning needs. The actual assessment of needs is particularly difficult in an institutional setting because of the competitive tradition of schooling. Most adults learned long ago to be guarded in disclosing what might appear to be weaknesses. Knowles advises facilitators should be sensitive to the initial reluctance many learners exhibit when asked to assess their learning needs.

Setting goals. Whereas the facilitator's goals are concerned with process, the self-directed learner must translate learning needs into achievable learning objectives. The facilitator's responsibility is to assist each learner in converting needs to objectives that are "clear, feasible, at appropriate levels of specificity or generality, personally meaningful, and measurable as to accomplishment" (p. 36). The key word is assist and not impose. Imposition negates the self-directed aspect of the whole endeavor.

Designing a learning plan. The greatest help a facilitator can provide someone new to self-directed learning experiences is turning attention to the collaborative nature of the group. By using group members as resources and, when appropriate, participating in a team approach to attacking problems, the self-directed learner can begin to unlearn the behaviors associated with membership in a competitive group. The facilitator can also assist in listing alternative methods for achieving objectives. Choosing from several options may be new to learners whose only experience has been in teacher-directed classrooms. The facilitator can help the learner become familiar with the various options and assist in developing a learning plan appropriate to the learner's objectives.

Engaging in learning activities. The facilitator may be asked to transmit content for some learners and thereby play, temporarily, the conventional role of teacher.

More likely, however, the facilitator will act as consultant to individuals or small inquiry groups. The climate should be such that individuals feel free to avail themselves of both roles, when appropriate. Knowles suggests the role of "process consultant" is critical for facilitators. This role provides assistance to learners in the process of the inquiry. The objective for a process consultant is to help learners feel more confident in their proceeding toward problem solution.

Evaluating learning outcomes. If the needs, objectives, and learning plan phases of the self-directed activity were clear, the evaluation part should have been anticipated early on. Mutually agreed upon criteria and/or methods of evaluation will be used to assess the actual learning. Peer review or feedback, again reflecting the collaborative climate of the classroom, can be useful to both the facilitator and the learner when evaluating the self-directed learning effort. Knowles includes over a dozen rating instruments that can be used by individuals or small groups to assist in the assessment of learning (pp. 113–128).

Developing a Learning Contract

Learners and facilitators can profit from the use of learning contracts. Learners benefit because the contract provides an opportunity to state explicitly what needs will be addressed through what learning strategies and assessed by what evaluation procedures. Facilitators find the learning contracts convenient tools for keeping track of the various needs, strategies, etc. the learners will be pursuing. The contracts can serve as records of past experiences and accomplishments as well as plans for future activities. Experience with many learning contracts enables facilitators to use them as examples for learners who are unfamiliar with their use.

A learning contract can take many forms. Knowles recommends one that contains columns for "Learning Objectives," "Learning Resources and Strategies," "Evidence of Accomplishment of Objectives," and "Criteria and Means for Validating Evidence." Within a classroom setting, Knowles suggests specified objectives be listed by the facilitator. These "given" objectives pertain to the course content as seen by the facilitator. In addition, a list of references appropriate to the content and a list of "inquiry units" that specify the kinds of questions the course is designed to pursue also should be provided the learners. From this course syllabus that includes objectives, references, and units of inquiry, each learner constructs a model of competence. (Knowles suggests how different grades can be contracted for; depending on the level of performance a learner is willing to achieve.) Learning objectives are determined by matching one's present level with the model's level and assessing the difference. Once all the columns are completed, each learner shares the contract wth a consultation team of three or four peers selected by the learner. The team reviews the contract and, if necessary, suggests changes. After being revised in light of the team's recommendations, the contracts are submitted to the facilitator for comments and possible changes.

After the process of peer and facilitator review, the contract is followed. It may require small group inquiry, independent inquiry or both. Kowles cautions that contracts can become constraints or in other ways become inappropriate and may need to be renegotiated after learning activities begin.

Commentary

Knowles' conception of self-directed learning is no different from Tough's in that both actually describe self-directed education, i.e., the management of learning resources.

The use of an idealized model with which to compare one's current level of competence is similar to Nadler's CEM approach that utilizes an ideal worker, against which the performance of the current worker is compared. In the critical events model, however, the ideal is determined by the organization and not the individual learner.

A tolerance for ambiguity may be nowhere more important than in the consideration of self-directed learning within an institutional setting. Some might consider the two terms mutually exclusive, but Knowles attempts to bridge the gap between conventional schooling and the new role of facilitator of learning by discussing the new competencies required of facilitator and learner. The negotiation between facilitator and learner is paramount in the learning contract process. Control over ends and means is intended to be mutual, not one-sided. Brookfield (1986) refers to this process as a transactional encounter (p. 20) between learner and facilitator. It is during this encounter when facilitators reveal their values regarding the persistent problem of simply responding to a learner's expressed needs or imposing some predetermined goal, irrespective of the learner's needs.

Knowles' prescriptions of how to facilitate self-directed learning contrast sharply with the institutional models of HRD and vocational training, but that is to be expected because their purposes are different. The degree to which a model is internally consistent with regard to its purpose may be the most important criterion for judging its worth. And when curriculum models purport to be generic, as those in the next section, it becomes quite difficult to judge them because they are tied to no single purpose.

SECTION VII

GENERIC MODELS

E fforts to generalize curriculum development procedures to all forms of adult education are considered here to be generic models. The efforts understandably are ambitious undertakings because the field of adult education is so diverse. One could argue it is not a field at all, but simply a set of practices, themselves disparate, and any attempt to find unifying threads or themes would be doomed from the beginning.

In order to accommodate the varied instances of the practice of adult education, designers of generic models typically qualify their prescriptions with caveats. These qualifications are necessary to match the peculiarities of specific settings, e.g., vocational/technical schools, public libraries, and continuing education workshops. But the concessions to unique aspects of some settings can detract from the overall design so much that it is rendered less useful as a guide for practice.

A great deal of judgment is necessary, therefore, when using a generic model to guide practice. Because of its intended universality, the various elements of a model may be of more or less utility, depending on the specific conditions that exist within any educational setting. This shortcoming of generic models must be balanced against the economy of effort they represent. Unfortunately, as in most judgments pertaining to education, there are no clear-cut guidelines to help make the decisions regarding the usefulness of a model.

CHAPTER 12

Houle's Model*

The approach Houle takes to develop his model is two dimensional. The first dimension is a cutting across of all forms of adult education to reveal eleven separate categories. The categories are determined not by outward appearance, but instead by "the source of authority and direction so far as planning and control are concerned" (p. 42).

Eleven Categories

The eleven categories are spread across four divisions. Each division is different in terms of control of procedure or intended audience. Table 12.1 contains the four divisions and eleven categories. Houle's contention is that too much energy has been wasted arguing about the relative merits of one of the eleven categories over another. He asserts the central question is not "Which is better than the other?" but should be "In what circumstances is one category better than another?"

"The process of education is strongly influenced by the nature of the category in which it is conducted" (p. 45). Houle provides specific illustrations of process within each of the eleven categories. He underscores the importance of category by illustrating the different processes, for example, that are inherent in C-3 and C-4. He declares,

---

*For a more detailed account of this model see Houle, C.O (1972). Unless otherwise indicated, all references in this chapter are to this source.

INDIVIDUAL

C-1   An individual designs an activity for himself

C-2   An individual or a group designs an activity for another individual

GROUP

C-3   A group (with or without a continuing leader) designs an activity for itself

C-4   A teacher or a group of teachers designs an activity for, and often with, a group of students

C-5   A committee designs an activity for a larger group

C-6   Two or more groups design an activity which will enhance their combined programs of service

INSTITUTION

C-7   A new institution is designed

C-8   An institution designs an activity in a new format

C-9   An institution designs a new activity in an established format

C-10   Two or more institutions design an activity which will enhance their combined programs of service

MASS

C-11   An individual, group, or institution designs an activity for a mass audience

Table 12.1   *Major Categories of Educational Design Stiuations (Howle, 1972, p. 44)*

Neither category is inherently superior to the other, but the two are different from one another in establishing both the ends and means of the learning process. That difference is particularly sharply felt when a group believes itself to be in one situation (category) and its leader believes himself to be in the other (pp. 45–46).

Houle advises that the categories are dynamic, not static, and that the educational planner

... examines the milieu in which he works, defines or chooses what appears to be the most logical or productive situation, identifies the category in which it falls, and shapes or guides his work in terms of the distinctive nature of that category (p. 91).

A final caveat Houle suggests is that the differences between categories are not always sharp and clear. Because of this ambiguity, leaders and participants may disagree on choice of appropriate procedures. Houle illustrates the difficulty in choosing in the case of a director of an evening college who wishes to inform the people of his community about urban problems.

> Should he use the group discussion approach (C-3), formal classwork (C-4), a conference (C-5), an all-community effort (C-10), or a lecture series (C-11) (p. 129)?

The decision should be made, Houle claims, on the basis of how specific goals will be influenced by the choice of a particular category and what resources are available to undertake any of the categories.

Development of Program Design

The second dimension of Houle's model is a series of decision points and components that constitute an adult education framework. Figure 12.1 represents the framework. Before describing each of the decision points and components, it is necessary to consider two generalizations regarding the model.

First, it will become clear when applying any part of the model to the various categories that some parts may play a lesser role than others. In C-1, for example, when a learner plans an educational activity, the concern for a "leader" in the endeavor is different from a C-4 situation, in which the leader is likely to be a professional educator.

The second generalization is that "the components are to be understood as a complex of interacting elements not as a logical sequence of steps" (p. 46). The model is described in a logical order, for the sake of clarity, but can be entered at any stage and pursued in any order dictated by the particular circumstances.

A possible educational activity is identified. There is no limit to the ways in which an individual or a group can become aware of a possible educational activity. The source of the idea may be external or internal to the individual or group. It may evolve out of a specific situation, as when an informal group meets and decides to create a

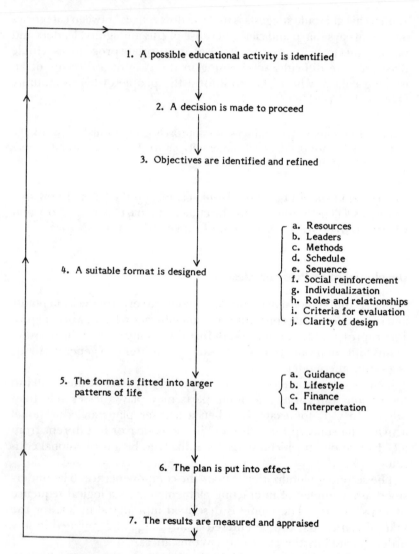

Figure 12.1   *A Generic Curriculum Model (Houle, 1972, p. 47).*

lecture series, or it can be a response to a felt need an individual experiences.

Houle delineates the possibilities for an educational activity entering the consciousness of an individual:

> As people think about themselves, they develop desires, grow dissatisfied with their lives, realize their lacks of ability, see disparities between present and desired accomplishments, sense their needs to grow in capacity or usefulness, and distinguish in many other ways between what might be and what is (p. 133).

The potential educational activity might be identified as a result of this self-knowledge or it might precipitate it.

A snapshot of an individual group or society would reveal many forms of educational activities present. Identifying or recognizing them as opportunities for learning usually is necessary to understanding the next phase of the model. However, it bears repeating that moving through the model from point 1 to point 7 is undertaken only for the ease of description, and that entry can (and is) made at any point in actual practice.

A decision is made to proceed. Frequently the decision to proceed is part of the identification process. It may be that when a person becomes aware of an educational activity the decision to participate is not considered a separate judgment. It is separated here in order to understand better the dynamics of the decision-making process and because, at other times, the decision is distinguished from the simple awareness of an activity.

Houle claims that in the majority of instances of identification of an educational activity, the decision is not to proceed. Invitations to join educational enterprises one receives through the mail or from the mass media are turned down more often than accepted. Houle notes:

> The decision about proceeding is usually a matter of subjective judgment, for it is impossible to demonstrate in advance that either a positive or a negative choice will be wise, considered either in its own terms or as the best of alternatives. Those who make the choice must try to consider all aspects of the situation and then, on balance, decide what to do (p. 136).

Typically individuals operate without benefit of codified policies to help them make such decisions. Unfortunately, many institutions likewise make decisions about offering educational programs in the absence of policy or guiding principle. Even with policy based on principle, interpretations have to be made with regard to specific applications and those interpretations are always subjective.

Objectives are identified and refined. Understanding objectives and the role they play in educational activities is a complex undertaking. Houle cites two reasons for the difficulty in analyzing objectives: One is that "they are always at the heart of an activity, not on its surface" (p. 137) and the other is that objectives are "defined by the simultaneous interaction of six factors" (p. 143).

Houle begins his discussion of objectives by differentiating them from motives and aspirations. "A motive is an inciting cause which helps to determine an individual's choice of an objective and his behavior in seeking it" (p. 138). But motives can be different from announced objectives. The difference is attested to by the research that reveals participants in courses, for example, state for their motives such reasons as escaping from routine and meeting new people (Johnston and Rivera, 1965, pp. 146–50. Cited by Houle, pp. 138–9).

An aspiration is strong desire for realization of ideals. "It exists only as a conception in the mind of either learner or educator" (p. 139). An individual's aspiration may be well thought out from philosophic positions or simply derived from surface values.

In contrast to both motive and aspiration, "an objective is an intended result of an educational activity" (p. 139). Objectives, according to Houle, do not exist "until the decision is made to take action, and it is then the effect sought by that action" (p. 139). Motives then are reasons for behaving and aspirations are ideals toward which people move. Objectives are found within educational activities and have a number of attributes that affect their quality. Houle discusses seven attributes of objectives.

Embedded within an educational activity, but not dormant, objectives have the following characteristics:

Objectives are:
- Rational—they impose a logical pattern;
- Practical—they are achievable;
- Pluralistic—they reflect more than a single outcome;
- Hierarchical—some are subsumed by others;
- Discriminative—they dictate some actions and rule out other actions; and
- Changeable over time—learners and teachers are affected by

the educational experience and consequently adjust their objectives accordingly.

Once objectives are differentiated from motives and aspirations, and seen as having a number of attributes, the discussion turns to understanding how objectives are affected by the interaction of six factors.

An educational activity has at least six factors operating on it. One is the *milieu*—the social and physical context in which the activity takes place. The *learners* represent another factor. *Content* or subject matter must be considered. The *design* of the content is a factor. The *aspirations* of the educators as well as of the learners are present. And finally, the *motives* of educators and learners play a part in the activity. Houle claims the interaction of these factors will determine the objectives and the format. A change in one will necessitate an adjustment in another, thereby affecting the nature of the objectives.

Oftentimes objectives reflect just one of the six factors. Houle contends all six factors must be considered and while that is seen by him as being possible, he advises, "the meshing is a creative process, having to do with the capacity of individuals and groups to weigh and evaluate available information and to establish priorities based on the assessment of present and future conditions" (p. 146).

Having objectives of an educational activity made explicit accomplishes a number of purposes. When objectives are known, they can help to shape the format, provide a description of the activity, clarify the thinking of planners and learners, and provide a sense of unity. Some negative consequences of having explicitly stated objectives can result from forgetting that such objectives contain abstractions. For example, changes in behavior which the objectives describe may not include all of the changes that could be indications of learning. Objectives tend to focus only on what can be measured. Exclusive concern with objectives could divert attention from the learning that is intended.

Houle suggests three types of objectives. One is the expected outcome or change in behavior. Another is objectives stated as principles that guide process. And the third type is facilitative, i.e., objectives that affect the format of the design. Whatever type of objective is used, Houle encourages its cooperative development. In nearly every category of educational design situations, opportunities are present for mutual (educator and learner) consideration of the nature of objectives, the factors affecting them and their eventual development and refinement.

A suitable format is designed. The format includes the ten elements listed in Figure 12.1. It is a blend of these elements that ultimately characterizes the entire educational activity. Houle emphasizes two points regarding the format. One is that the order in which the elements are considered will depend on the context in which the activity is being planned and the inherent characteristics of the activity itself. The other point of emphasis is that education is a cooperative act. He urges collaboration between planners and participants whenever possible to assure understanding as well as increased likelihood of acceptance of the format. Each of the ten elements in Figure 12.1 will be described below with the understanding that their order and separate discussion are for the sake of clarity and not reflective of relative importance or sequence of attention. Furthermore, many of the elements interact with one another and affect the overall format accordingly.

Resources. Selecting learning resources requires judgment about the specific situation, goals, learners, and other relevant factors. A resource can be "any object, person, or other aspect of the environment which can be used for support or help in an educational activity" (p. 152). Some resources dictate the method to be used with them, e.g., books and reading, films and viewing. The professional literature contains empirical studies and anectdotal accounts of various learning resources and their advantages and disadvantages. Generalizations across many settings are tenuous. Houle's advice is to use the practical wisdom that comes from experience and insights gained from the literature to make judicious choices of appropriate learning resources.

Leaders. Oftentimes referred to a teachers or facilitators, leaders are the ones directly responsible for assisting learners in achieving their objectives. But, unlike conventional K-12 schooling or even the majority of higher education institutions, there is no well developed cadre of personnel who see themselves as adult educators. Instead, many of the leaders in adult education settings are something else first, be that librarian, skilled mechanic, high school English teacher or whatever. The choice of a leader then may include consideration of other factors that typically do not have much effect on other teachers. One frequent impact the leader has is on the methods that will be used with or for the learners.

Methods. Many methods exist that will assist learners in achieving their educational objectives. Houle contends that leaders are a major factor in determining methods because they may be limited in which methods can be used effectively. Other factors affecting the choice of method will be the objectives being sought, the amount of time available, the number of learners involved, the availability of resources, and the learners' preferences. Because no one method has been found to be superior, a variety of methods should be employed as long as consideration of other factors does not rule out any one of them.

Schedule. "Most present decisions about scheduling are determined by tradition, necessity, the best available judgment, or an arbitrary choice among alternatives" (p. 161). The challenge to adult educators is to fit a schedule of educational activites into the complex life patterns of adults. Establishing a schedule that simply reflects the arbitrary requirements of an institution and failing to take into consideration the objectives, resources, and needs of the learners is as unwise as it is commonplace.

Sequence. The order in which content is learned is called sequence. Despite a great deal of attention to this element, there are no hard and fast rules regarding the "best" sequence of any content. A general guide is to start where the learner is and proceed from there. Houle's summary of the issues associated with sequence acknowledges the dangers of being too extreme in either direction. "It is equally wrong for a teacher to be so true to content that he ignores the abilities and desires of his students and for him to be so concerned with their wishes and feelings that he forgets or denies content" (p. 162).

Social reinforcement. Except for self-directed learning (C-1) and mass audience appeal (C-11) most learning situations have a social dimension. The interaction of various personalities assembled for a common purpose can create an ethos or feeling of group identity. Houle advises collaboration between leader and learners in designing the various elements of format to assure a positive social climate. In general, learning is enhanced by positive social reinforcement.

Individualization. Whenever possible, educational planners should try to accommodate the individual needs and abilities of each learner. That, of course, is a tall order, and the complexity of education, the size of the group, and length of time available for such accommodations are barriers to individualization.

Roles and relationships. Roles are the expected behavior of individuals in a situation and affect relationships with others. People play different roles, depending on the situation. Educator and learner, for example, are two different roles and the expected behavior from each is different, especially in a conventional K-12 school setting. With adults, however, where collaboration may be encouraged with regard to choices of format, the roles can become blurred and possibly cause confusion in both leaders and learners. It may be necessary, therefore, to be explicit about certain behavior expectations to reduce the ambiguity and frustration often associated with acting "outside" one's perceived role.

Criteria for evaluation. Definition and form of design are enhanced, according to Houle, by the inclusion of "a statement of the criteria which from the beginning seem to offer the best available indications of success" (p. 171). The standards, rules, or tests that will be used to assess learning should be designated before an educational activity is begun. Establishing criteria beforehand, however, does not preclude changing them as the activity proceeds but not having evaluative criteria in the beginning will make it difficult to structure the other elements of format.

Clarity of design. The particular arrangement of all the elements of format constitute what is called the design. Houle advises helping learners understand exactly what the design entails so they can see clearly where the activities are leading, the appropriate role expectations, and criteria by which learning will be measured, as well as the relationship of these elements to the other elements of format. When learners are aware of a clear design, they are more likely to experience success in the total educational activity.

The format is fitted into larger patterns of life. Learners, educators, and the staff of an institution are involved in this stage of program planning. The learners must adjust their schedules and priorities to accommodate the educational activity. The educators must consider the influence of the activity on their lives, as well as how it may affect the learners. The institution, through its staff, must make provisions for planning, coordinating, promoting, and recruiting, all in the name of the educational activity being developed. Houle notes these activities frequently occur "out of order," and though they can be described as if they are in a rational order, they usually take place simultaneously, and many times, while the elements of format are being considered. Houle includes four elements under the heading of "fitting format into life patterns;" guidance; life style; finance; and interpretation.

Guidance. Providing information about requirements, fees, and schedules is a minimal effort at providing service. Guidance, according to Houle, includes taking a sincere interest in the learner's needs and interests and usually involves interpersonal relationships that likely exceed the competence levels of typical staff employed as counselors. Until professional counselors are in place, he advises using a common-sense approach to helping learners discover their needs and avoiding problems that require in-depth personal counseling.

Houle suggests adult educators reexamine the assumptions that adults know what they want and that they would resist efforts to guide them in or out of educational activities. Making information available that can aid an adult assess needs and help to match those needs with appropriate educational activities is a continuing challenge to those responsible for providing guidance to learners.

Life style. Unlike conventional K-12 schooling that virtually constitutes the life style of the young, adult education activities require conscious adjustment in the life styles of the participating adults. Houle observes, "Education is never simply added to the actions of a life; it replaces something else; and that replacement must be carefully considered both when an activity is planned and throughout its duration" (p. 177).

Finance. Educational activities can be financed from a number of sources. The most common sources are taxation, student fees, and public or private grants. If student fees are involved, the planners need to consider the impact such a financial burden may have on the potential students. Houle claims the problem of financing adult education from an institution's perspective takes one of three forms: inadequacy of funding; unrealistic expectations in spending grant monies too quickly, with insufficient planning; and unstable funding patterns.

Interpretation. The planners of an educational activity need to interpret the activity to the public. This is a kind of public relations that serves to legitimize both the institution's offering the activity and the learner's taking advantage of it.

The planner's responsibility for interpretation is even more critical when working within a category that includes an institution trying to introduce a wholly new format. Houle contrasts the need for interpretation of adult education programs with similar situations in welfare, health, and recreation where there exists a general social understanding of their importance, requiring little if any need for interpretation.

The plan is put into effect. Some plans cannot be implemented fully until leaders and learners meet. An educational activity that involves problem solving on an individual basis, for example, requires learners be present to reveal the particular problems to be solved. Activities within sensitivity groups evolve as the interaction of participants occurs, thus precluding specific planning in any kind of detail.

But even activities that can be planned legitimately in advance often are modified to accommodate the realities of the specific situation.

Houle suggests it should be "expected that however well-laid the original plans may be, they will almost at once require changes, since even the most experienced educator or learner working within a well-established framework can never foresee all of the contingencies which must be cared for" (p. 181). A realistic approach is to begin putting the plan into effect and expect to make constant readjustments.

The results are measured and appraised. Evaluation of the activity ought to involve both measurement, which usually incorporates some kind of objectivity, and appraisal, which requires a more subjective assessment of the whole activity. Many educators and learners have a propensity for measuring anything that can be measured and therefore need to guard against the fallacy that suggests, "If it can be measured it must be important." Houle suggests a combination of measurement and appraisal that helps to answer the following questions:

1. How well was each objective achieved?
2. If I did better than expected, why?
3. Was the goal too high or was the design poorly planned and executed?
4. If the latter, what specifics were wrong?
5. If the objective was reached would I have done better if I had set higher levels of accomplishment?
6. If goals changed during the course of learning, should they have?
7. What additional criteria of evaluation should have been used?
8. Can I make an estimate of how well I would have done on them (p. 184)?

The evaluation of an educational activity requires subjectivity—even when "objective" measures are used. As long as evaluators remain sensitive to the value judgments involved in an appraisal, there should be little chance for misinterpretation.

Repeating the educational cycle. Figure 12.1 contains a long line from the bottom moving to the top. This line indicates the application of all that is learned from one educational activity to the planning of the next. As appraisal occurs, for example, one can begin anticipating the next activity and incorporating relevant insights from one to the other. Both leaders and learners go through this process and the wise ones profit from each experience.

Commentary

Houle precedes his generic model with a consideration of basic structures and functions the adult education enterprise encompasses. By attending first to his eleven categories, moving from self-directed learning (C-1) to planning for a mass audience (C-11) he calls attention to and places an order upon the myriad forms of adult education. His approach emphasizes structure more than function because nearly any of the eleven categories can serve different purposes.

The generic model is adaptable to all eleven categories. The model is comprehensive and includes all possible considerations. In terms of emphasis, less attention is placed on determining needs of learners or matching activities vis á vis learners' needs. But even this generalization is tenuous because Houle emphasizes throughout his discussion of the model that various aspects (including individualization) may receive more attention than others, depending on each unique situation.

The degree to which adult education is situation-specific may be related to the validity of any generalizations about creating or gaining access to knowledge and skills. Houle's model can, at the very least, serve as a checklist for planners to assure they do not overlook any aspects critical to curriculum planning.

CHAPTER 13

Boone's Conceptual Programming Model*

T he conceptual programming model advanced by Boone (1985) is
based on assumptions, concepts, and the actual experiences of
adult educators as change agents and programmers. It is intended
for both formal and nonformal contexts and, according to Boone,
"can be applied anywhere there is a need for adults to engage in
educational activities in fulfilling personal or group needs" (p. 218).
Table 13.1 contains the conceptual programming model.

Boone's conceptual programming model includes three major subprocesses: planning, design/implementation, and evaluation/account-
ability. Each of these subprocesses is built upon certain assumptions
and concepts and includes a number of processual tasks. The subprocesses, assumptions, and tasks are interrelated, but will be described separately in order to better understand the specific elements
of the model.

Planning

Within an organizational context, (Boone presupposes such a context in describing his model), the relationship of planning to the organization is reciprocal. Planning is imperative and,

---

*For a more detailed description of this model, see Boone *Developing Programs in Adult
Education* (1985). Unless otherwise indicated, all references in this chapter will be to
this source.

1. provides a legitimate road map for a rational response to un-
   certainty and change;
2. facilitates control of organizational operations by collecting information to analyze needs and evaluate its programs and services; and
3. orients the organization to a futuristic leadership stance (p. 80).

Boone defines planning as "a rational, continuing sequence of precise
educational activities carried out by adult educators, operating from
an organizational base, through which the organization establishes
and maintains linkage with learners and their leaders in collaborative
identification, assessment, and analysis of their educational needs" (p.
82).

Assumptions and Concepts Five assumptions and four concepts
undergird the subprocess of planning. The assumptions are:

1. Planning is a futuristic activity.
2. The planning behavior of the adult education organization is
   proactive rather than reactive.
3. Planning enhances efficiency in the adult education organization.
4. Planning is sequential or stepwise, involving collecting and analyzing related information, and identifying, assessing, and analyzing needs.
5. Planning is collaborative; that is, it includes representatives of
   all who are affected by it (p. 81).

The four concepts included in planning are: 1) planned change; 2)
linkage; 3) democracy; and 4) translation. *Planned change* "implies an
exactness for organizational planning activities" (p. 81). Boone emphasizes collaboration between adult educators and their target publics, wherein mutual goal setting, for example, is part of planned
change.

Linkage refers to target publics being involved, through their leaders
or learners, with an organization's efforts to identify, assess, and analyze the target publics' needs. The term encompasses the idea of collaboration and is descriptive of the goal that educational organizations
should seek to achieve.

The third concept associated with planning is *democracy*. It implies
an "open and free participation of learners in the decision-making
process . . ." (p. 81). Whereas planned change refers to the interest in
being specific about the future and linkage describes the sought after
state of relationship between an organization and its target publics,

PLANNING		DESIGN & IMPLEMENTATION		EVALUATION & ACCOUNTABILITY
The Organization & its Renewal Process	Linking the Organization to its Publics	Designing the Planned Program	Implementing the Planned Program	

Understanding of and Commitment to Functions of the Organization
  Mission
  Philosophy
  Objectives
	Study, Analysis, and Mapping of the Organization's Publics	Translating Expressed Needs into Macro Needs	Developing Plans of Action	Determining and Measuring Program Outputs

Understanding and Commitment to the Organization's Structure
  Roles
  Relationships
	Identifying Target Publics	Translating Macro Needs Into Macro Objectives	Translating Needs into Teaching Objectives	Assessing Program Inputs

Knowledge About and Skilled in Organization's Processes
  Supervision
  Staff Development
  Evaluation and Accountability
	Identifying and Interfacing with Leaders of Target Publics	Specifying General Educational Strategies and Learning Activities	Specifying Learning Experiences for each Teaching Objective	Using Evaluation Findings for Program Revisions, Organizational Renewal, and for Accounting to Publics, Parent Organization, Funding Sources, the Profession, and where appropriate, the Governance Body

Understanding of and Commitment to a Tested Conceptual Framework for Programming	Collaborative Identification, Assessment, and Analysis of Needs Specific to Target Publics	Specifying Macro Outcomes of the Planned Program	Developing Plans for Evaluating Learner Outcomes and Assessing Learning Experiences	
Understanding and Commitment to Continuous Organizational Renewal			Developing and Implementing Strategies and Techniques for Marketing the Plans of Action	
			Developing and Following Through on Plans to Recruit and Train Leader-Learner Resources	
			Monitoring and Reinforcing the Teacher-Learner Transaction	

Table 13.1   *A Conceptual Programming Model (Boone, 1985, p. 61)*

democracy speaks to the nature of the process engaged in by the adult educators and leaders when planning.

The fourth concept undergirding planning is *translation*. This involves a reciprocal relationship between the adult educator and the public to be served. The characteristics of each party, i.e., the adult educator's values, knowledge, and methodology and the particular public's social and cultural environment, must be understood by both parties if collaborative planning is to be successful. "Translating goals, beliefs, values, norms, and other aspects so that differences and commonalities can be recognized and appreciated is the adult educator's responsibility," according to Boone (p. 82). The definition of planning includes the organization and its linkage with target publics. Each of these two dimensions is addressed in the model through a series of processual tasks. A processual task is "an orderly set of actions engaged in by adult educators in applying a concept to a particular situation . . ." (p. 82).

The Organization and its Renewal Process Table 13.1 indicates five elements under the heading of the organization and its renewal process. The focus of each element is the quality of relationship of the adult educator to his or her organization.

Understanding of and commitment to the organization's mission, philosophy and objectives. The total adult education staff of an organization, according to Boone, must understand and be committed to the mission, philosophy, and objectives of the organization it serves. The mission of an organization speaks to its nature and distinguishing characteristics. A mission statement, for example, could include descriptions of the organization's "origin, legal basis, clientele, reasons for existence, and types of programs to be generated" (p. 85).

The philosophy of the organization is what Boone calls its "value framework." He contends "the philosophy of an educational organization reflects the firm conviction that people adjust to change most rapidly in a democratic environment in which self-expression, self-direction, and self-improvement are encouraged" (p. 85). Such a democratic environment is best achieved, he claims, through a continuing education program in which people take the initiative in identifying and solving their own problems. The organization should support this effort and encourage its members to be committed to it.

An outgrowth of mission and philosophy is the organization's objectives. On a macrolevel, the objectives "have their origin in the contemporary needs of (the organization's) publics and constitute the framework within which all decisions and actions about the organization's program must be linked" (p. 85). The various job groups within an organization will have their own, more specific objectives and all members of all job groups should understand what these objectives are. The route to understanding the organization's objectives is through continuous involvement of staff members in their formulation and refinement.

Understanding and commitment to the organization's structure. In order to achieve the macro objectives of the educational organization, it is necessary that staff members understand their individual roles and how these roles are related to both their job group's roles and the overall role of the organization. Too little attention, according to Boone, has typically been given to linking the various roles within one organization to its objectives.

Knowledgeable about and skillful in supervision, staff development, and evaluation and accountability. The educational organization must be dynamic in order to respond to the changing needs of its target publics. The dynamic quality is achieved by providing opportunities for continuous self-renewal of its staff members. Boone recommends supervisory styles that recognize the need for self-renewal and provide opportunities and support for maintaining it. In addition, the adult educator should be committed to evaluation and accountability.

Evaluation entails the following three processes:

1. measure the behavioral changes that result;
2. provide measures of effective application of learned behavior in real life situations; and
3. provide some measure of whether or not desired changes have occurred in the social and economic patterns of relevant publics (p. 87).

Before accountability can be fully achieved an evaluative system containing these three processes must be in place. Accountability involves more than evaluation; it includes a summary of needs identification, program design and implementation, an evaluation system, and a process by which all of this relevant information can be disseminated to those to whom the organization is accountable.

Understand and become committed to a tested conceptual framework for programming. The very nature of a conceptual programming model, i.e., that it is based on certain assumptions, concepts, and processes, permits testing any of the action steps that are prescribed for planning, designing and implementing, and evaluating and accounting. Boone believes adult educators should continually challenge and test the conceptual model used by their organization in order to make whatever adjustments are necessary to improve the model's effectiveness.

Understand and become committed to continuous organizational renewal. Organizational renewal is related to keeping current with the societal and target groups' needs. As needs change, the organization should change as well. It is incumbent upon adult educators working within an organization to remain sensitive to the changing environment in which their organization functions.

Linking the Organization to its Publics Programs for adults should have their origin in the needs of the publics being served. Determining those needs, according to Boone, "is the most challenging, perplexing, and necessary task confronting the professional adult educator" (p. 89).

Study, analysis, and mapping of the organization's publics. In order to secure the attention, interest, and commitment of a target group to change its behavior as a result of educational programs, it is imperative that those programs be based on the target group's needs. Boone observes:

> Needs are determined by a multitude of psychological, social, and cultural factors. The origin and intensity of such needs are related or linked to systems of patterned interaction and processes of socialization through which humankind acquires a distinctive lifestyle (p. 89).

The adult educator must become knowledgeable about the psychological, social, and cultural forces that influence the development of needs. In addition, educators should be aware of the various social, political, and economic groupings in the society. It is important to needs analysis that these groupings become visible to the adult educator. Typically the members of these groups (the target publics) share certain goals, beliefs, values, attitudes, and customs. It is assumed, furthermore, that the goals, beliefs, values, etc. for various target publics are different. All of which suggests the adult educator remain alert and sensitive to these differences. The same program that works well for one group may not work at all for another group.

Boone discusses four conceptual tools necessary for effective analysis and mapping of the organization's publics: 1) social system analysis; 2) social stratification; 3) social differentiation; and 4) cultural analysis. In his discussion of what constitutes a community he delineates five characteristics: 1) a group of people; 2) shared interests, attitudes, and activities; 3) common identity; 4) frequent and continuing interaction; and 5) living in an identifiable territory or space that can be mapped. Finally, he lists examples of communities that can be identified by virtue of certain functions:

Political community: county, township, and city governments; political organizations.
Educational community: schools-primary, secondary, vocational, colleges, universities; nonformal education.
Mass communication community: TV, newspapers, radio.
Economic community: employment, industry, business, finance (p. 99).

Each of these communities could yield smaller, more homogeneous groups. Homogeneity is relative, of course, in that many groups will overlap.

The entire mapping process is predicated upon the assumption that relatively homogeneous groups of people live within the environment of the adult education organization. The groups that are mapped may overlap, but are identified, roughly at least, as potential target publics of the educational organization.

Identifying target publics. The target publics to be served by the organization will be determined by several variables. The mission statement and objectives may assign priority to the groups to be served. The particular resources of the organization help determine the rank order of target publics. Finally, the law may require certain groups to have educational programs.

Whatever process is used, the targeted publics should be ranked and resources should be marshalled to equip the organization to fulfill its mission. The ranking, incidentally, is itself a function of the times, in that needs can change and adjustments are made accordingly. Assuming a list of target publics is established, the next step is identifying and working with the leaders of the groups.

Identifying and interfacing with leaders of target publics. Boone discusses five approaches to identifying formal and informal leaders of target publics: 1) positional; 2) reputational; 3) personal influence or opinion leadership; 4) decision making; and 5) social participation approaches. Each approach has advantages and disadvantages and Boone recommends an eclectic approach that draws from any or all of the five, depending on the situation and resources available. The assumption is that the leaders reflect the belief and values of the target public and, because of their leadership role, whether formal or informal, will greatly affect the success of an adult education effort aimed at "their" target public.

The next task is to interact with the leader in order to "meld the provider system with the potential user system" (p. 109). Boone suggests the initial meetings between the adult educator and the identified leader be informal and characterized as conversations wherein the leader is dominant and the adult educator is listening more than talking. Two immediate goals are sought at this juncture: 1) building a sense of trust and 2) beginning a collaborative approach to viewing needs.

Collaborative identification, assessment, and analysis of needs specific to target pubics. Identification of needs is, according to Boone, "the most important facet of adult education . . ." (p.113) Boone reviews several approaches to working with leaders in identifying a group's needs and concludes that all support the aim of beginning with needs in establishing adult education programs.

The concept of need has been addressed frequently in the professional literature. Boone summarizes his review of needs with the following definition:

> . . . needs of a person or a group of persons who make up a target public are the cumulative effects of a host of psychological, social, cultural, and physiological factors. Thus, needs can be defined as a deficiency, imbalance, lack of adjustment, or gap between the present situation and a set of societal norms believed to be more desirable (pp. 114–115).

The determination of needs then involves two decisions: 1) what needs are important? and 2) how will information be gathered to justify a program that responds to the needs?

Deciding which needs are important "can be determined from social norms, research findings, and value judgments by adult educators and the leaders of target publics" (p. 116). Once the needs are agreed upon, the next step is collecting information that will permit diagnosing them. Boone asserts "the target publics and their leaders make the final judgment about educational needs and what will fulfill those needs" (p. 118). Five approaches to collecting information about needs are discussed by Boone: 1) interfacing with leaders; 2) listening; 3) survey approach; 4) community/target public study; and 5) census or other survey reports. The important element in whatever approach is used is the involvement of the leaders and potential learners in diagnosing needs. When agreement is reached on what needs are important and the present condition of the target public is assessed, the next step is designing and implementing programs that address them.

Design and Implementation

Boone characterizes the intellectual process of the planning stage as inductive, whereas the design and implementation stage requires deductive thinking. Beginning with the needs identified and analyzed in the planning process, the task for the adult educator is to translate those needs into programs that address them.

The needs may have to be ordered, from most important to least, and that too is done collaboratively with the target public's leaders and learners. But the leadership for program planning rests primarily on the adult educators as they begin designing suitable learning experiences.

Assumptions and Concepts The primary assumption is "that all educational activity is aimed at bringing about individual behavioral change" (p. 129). In addition, Boone lists eight other assumptions relevant to the design and implementation subprocess:

1. The planned program is the adult education organization's principal means of responding to the needs of its target publics.
2. The planned program is a blueprint of major behavioral changes to be effected by the adult education organization over a relatively long period of time, if improvements are to be noted in these publics.
3. The planned program provides the adult education organization with a rationale for the allocation, deployment, and use of its resources.
4. The planned program serves as a guide and provides direction for decisions on strategies for coping with the educational needs of learners.
5. The planned program provides the adult education organization with an excellent public relations tool.
6. The design of plans of action guides the systematic development of change strategies to deal with the needs and objectives enumerated in the planned program, within a relatively short period of time.
7. The planned program and plans of action provide the adult educator with the means needed to market them to the intended publics.
8. The planned program and plans of action provide a base for the adult educator in identifying, recruiting, and developing resource persons to assist with the actual implementation of the planned program and its accompanying plans of action (p. 129).

Two concepts alluded to in the assumptions are "time" and "plan of action," both of which have a special meaning in the design process. Length of time is a function of the gap between current level and ideal level regarding a specific need. The greater the gap, the longer the time required to satisfy the need. The plan of action refers to more specific plans that detail actual learning experiences. More will be said about plans of action later. Attention now is directed at the two levels of design, macro and micro, that characterize Boone's conceptual model.

The macro level of design is called the planned program level. It represents the overarching needs or goals toward which the more specific and focused plans of action are directed. The relatively specific needs and objectives associated with plans of action are at the micro level. Descriptions of program design are at the macro level, whereas descriptions of implementation involve developing plans of action, which are at the micro level.

Translating expressed needs into macro needs. Assuming there is a needs hierarchy, an expressed need, according to Boone, is usually a lower level need that can be expanded, developmentally, to a higher level, macro need. He illustrates the process of translation with an example: If an expressed need is "consumers need to be more careful shoppers," the macro level of that need can be, "consumers need to make informed decisions in the marketplace that will provide them increased satisfaction and yield the greatest return in terms of funds expended" (p. 137). The macro need includes several micro level needs that are more specific and cumulatively contribute to the macro need.

Transmitting macro needs into macro objectives. Macro objectives are the terminal behaviors toward which the education plan is directed. The macro needs have corresponding macro objectives. In the case of the consumer cited above, the macro objective is "consumers to make informed decisions in the marketplace." Just as a macro need encompasses more specific micro needs, a macro objective includes more specific micro objectices.

The hierarchy of needs has a corresponding hierarchy of objectives. With regard to the objectives, Boone advises they must be:

- consistent with organizational mission;
- within the limitations of available resources; and
- practical within the capabilities of intended learners (p. 138).

Objectives indicate the desirable behavior the learners will be able to demonstrate as a result of the educational program. Objectives also "provide bases for the selection and organization of learning experiences, give direction, define goals for accomplishment, relate educational input and learning output, and make the specific process of learning mutually comprehensible for all involved" (pp. 140–141). Boone reemphasizes the need to state objectives in behavioral terms.

Specifying general educational strategies and learning activities. Boone defines strategy as "a carefully designed plan or scheme of learning activities to achieve the macro objective and its subordinate micro objectives" (p. 142). This element of the model anticipates the specific plans of action for achieving the micro objectives, but it addresses other concerns that precede actual teaching-learning experiences. The general strategy takes into account the overall design or approach indicated by the previous elements and establishes plans for delivery and recruitment of participants. The same kind of attention paid to a target public's social and cultural characteristics that aided the identification of needs is necessary here in helping to remove barriers to participation and promote the likelihood of a good fit between providers and consumers.

Specifying macro outcomes of the planned program. An extension of the macro objectives to a larger group or community is what is meant by macro outcomes. Whereas the macro and micro objectives have an individual as a target, the outcomes are the more general effects that might appear as a result of achieving the objectives. Anticipation of certain outcomes, which is a tentative exercise at best, is a necessary step toward evaluation and accountability, about which more will be said later.

Implementing the Planned Program Designing and using specific plans of action constitute the implementation of the planned program. "Plans of action mirror the process of designing the planned program, with the difference that allocated times for completion are shorter and specific objectives are more narrowly stated" (p. 147). The tasks associated with designing or developing plans of action involve the determination of micro needs and their corresponding objectives, selection of teaching strategies and learning experiences, and construction of specific plans for evaluating changes in learners' behavior. The process, according to Boone, is built upon rational curriculum development, a hierarchical approach to specifying objectives, and human developmental frameworks.

Translating needs into teaching objectives. Each macro need of the planned program is made up of a number of related, but more specific micro needs. These micro needs must be ordered into a logical hierarchy and then translated into micro objectives that become teaching-learning objectives of the plan of action. Boone recommends use of a two dimensional chart to display content aspects of objectives as row headings and behavioral aspects of the objectives as column headings. The analysis and display of objectives on such a chart provide three benefits: 1) it becomes evident that a single behavior may require knowledge about more than one content area; 2) the relationship of content to behavior is more clear; and 3) the selecting and sequencing of teaching-learning experiences are aided by the specification of content for each behavior.

Specifying learning experiences for each teaching objective. Boone discusses a number of generalizations about learning that should be considered when choosing or designing teaching-learning strategies. Motivation (extrinsic and intrinsic), practice, relearning, readiness, and self-directed approaches to learning are cited as important considerations in making decisions about strategies. Boone also emphasizes the importance of taking into account each individual's unique background and experience. Finally, he recommends three criteria to be used in organizing teaching-learning experiences: *continuity*—having learners recall and practice other elements of the curriculum; *sequence*—having each successive experience build on the previous one; and *integration*—having experiences organized in order to help learners acquire an increasingly unified understanding of the content. No specific formula exists for selecting or designing learning experiences. The generalizations and criteria should be considered in light of the specific target public's characteristics. The resulting learning experiences should be compatible with the individuals for whom they were planned.

Developing plans for evaluating learner outcomes and assessing learning experiences. The evaluation and accountability subprocess is anticipated at the plan of action stage by developing means by which the achievement of micro objectives is assessed. Boone claims the overall evaluation and accountability subprocess often falters because specific evaluation plans are not made part of the plans of action. Evaluating learning outcomes and assessing learning experiences can be aided by the use of the two-dimensional chart described earlier. Boone glancingly refers to the criteria of performance objectives, made popular by Mager (1975), that include a statement of the specific behavior, conditions under which it is exhibited, and a standard of performance.

Developing and implementing strategies and techniques for marketing the plans of action. Boone defines marketing in adult education as "gaining acceptance of, consensus upon, or participation in any given educational venture" (p. 157). Successful marketing of the plans of action and the overall program is dependent upon time, location, and costs to the participants. No formula will guarantee success, but continued involvement of a target public's leaders and learners in decisions about marketing will improve the chances of a program's acceptance. If the planning subprocess involved the target public's leaders and learners as outlined earlier, and the needs were identified collaboratively, the program that evolved should appeal to that target public.

Developing and following through on plans to recruit and train leader-learner resources. The plans of action, having been developed by this stage, must be analyzed to determine what kinds of specific teaching-learning activities will be used. The analysis will reveal what resources—human and material—will be needed in order to successfully implement the plans. Consideration of location and time also should be made now. Boone discusses a number of factors that can affect choice of site and scheduling of activities.

In addition to physical materials required for implementing the plans of action, the human resources must be determined, and, in the case of lay personnel, recruited and trained. Boone's observation is that the earlier subprocesses of planning and designing should have revealed leaders and learners from the target public who may be prospective candidates for assisting in the teaching or assuming greater responsibility for implementation of the plans of action. The specific teaching-learning activities will call for certain competencies that lay personnel may not have. The training of volunteers must be centered on the specific competencies dictated by the activities.

Monitoring and reinforcing the teacher-learner transaction. Boone recommends a participant-observer role for the adult educator who is monitoring the planned learner experiences. The role would permit first-hand observation of the activities, to ensure they are being implemented as planned, as well as availability to those conducting the activities, to provide assistance when needed. The adult educator's responsibility is to develop a system of monitoring that satisfies both the accountability aspect, i.e., are the activities being implemented as planned? and the resource aspect, i.e., is assistance available to supplement the activity leader's expertise, when necessary?

The system of monitoring should be characterized as a two way communication link between the adult educator and those responsible for actual implementation. The information gained from observing the teaching-learning activities, whether it be from the adult educator, a lay instructor, or resource person, should be considered by the adult educator so that adjustment decisions will assure maximum effectiveness.

Finally, reinforcement to adult learners who change their behavior as a result of the learning activities is crucial to sustaining the change. The adult educator may have to train lay leaders in the effective use of rewards for adult learners whose behaviors are being changed by the learning experience. The importance of the reinforcement is consistent with behavioristic learning theory.

Evaluation and Accountability

Evaluation is a continuous process in that it is anticipated throughout the model and it "closes the loop" of the program development cycle. A number of definitions of evaluation exists, and Boone discusses the differences, suggesting several themes that should permeate a definition of evaluation. Among the themes suggested are rationality and order, organizational context, and decision making based ultimately on judgments of what is good. Essentially, evaluation should answer questions about "how program inputs, context, and processes relate to program outputs; how efficient a program is; how suitable it is; and its overall importance" (p. 172).

Determining and measuring program outputs. Intended program outputs are the objectives that are agreed upon before the teaching-learning activities occur. Unintended outputs, by definition, are not specified ahead of time, but should be anticipated and assessed whenever possible. Outputs can be measured through tests or other observations of behavioral changes, including interviews and surveys, but Boone reminds that objectives must be observable and quantifiable.

Assessing program inputs. The evaluation of outputs is done with an eye to their relationship to the inputs. Materials and methods, used in teaching-learning experiences, for example, should be related to the specific objectives (outputs) of the program. One aspect of evaluation is to examine if and how such program inputs are related to outputs. Preceding the choice of methods and materials, decisions were made regarding objectives and needs. These decisions can be reviewed as well, in light of the output evaluations. And going back even further in the planning subprocess, the decisions that were made in identifying leaders of target publics and the original mapping of the target publics itself can be reexamined when program outputs are assessed. In effect, the entire model is checked during the evaluation subprocess.

Organizational renewal was considered originally under the subprocess of planning. Renewal becomes necessary whenever a target public's needs are met, because that changes the environment in which the organization operates. Evaluation, then, can be seen as a vital link in a chain of events that begins and ends with organizational renewal. The process is continual.

Accountability is the final subprocess of the conceptual model. Simply put, accountability means adult educators have the responsibility to "1) report evaluation results; 2) analyze the organization in terms of evaluation results; and 3) make recommendations, based on evaluation results, to their organization" (p. 198). Accountability reports, depending on the situation, could be submitted to the leaders or learners of a target public; the adult education organization that was responsible for the program; a funding source or governing body; and the professional adult education field itself. As an extension of evaluation, accountability is the formal means by which adult educators demonstrate professional responsibility for their plans and action.

Commentary

The conceptual programming model is one of the most comprehensive and detailed accounts of activities necessary for successful curriculum development. Several principles run throughout the model that provide consistent guides to action. Organizational renewal, systematic identification or target publics, collaborative planning, and hierarchical ordering of needs and corresponding objectives appear time and again to remind adult educators of the importance of consistently applying the conceptual constructs upon which the model is based.

The conceptual programming model is promoted as generic, i.e., applicable to many different settings, but has some obvious shortcomings. It presupposes an adult education organization as its base, which would appear to limit its application in non-educational settings such as business and industry.

The model's emphasis on behavioral objectives, rooted in Mager (1975) and Tyler (1971) disregards Tyler's more recent retreat from such specific behaviorism and critical assessment of Mager's influence, noted by Brookfield (1986, pp. 209–210). But even without Tyler's more humanistic reinterpretation of his original work, one should be sensitive to the inherent shortcomings of such exclusive reliance on behaviorism.

Especially with adults, for whom education oftentimes is more than acquiring new skills, it is legitimate to have objectives that are not amenable to being stated in behavioral terms. The conceptual programming model, like the generic competency-based vocational technical model described in Chapter 2, does not allow for anything but observable, quantifiable objectives.

Finally, Boone's approach to a needs based curriculum is direct. He encourages collaboration between the adult educator and the leaders of potential learners in negotiating higher-order needs. Determining needs is a value laden enterprise and Boone does not deny it. What is recommended as a guide is "to increase the level of socialization of these publics . . . to the extent that they become knowledgeable about, concerned with, and committed to the attainment of higher level or extrinsic needs" (p. 68). And he assumes that dialogue between the adult educator and the target leader/learner will resolve any conflicts between perceptions of needs. His assumption appears valid if the specific purpose of an activity is not counter to the leader/learner's purpose.

CHAPTER 14

Summary and Conclusions

The professional literature contains a number of adult education curriculum models. Some of these models are essentially single purpose in their design and promise, in effect, to serve this single purpose most effectively and efficiently. The purposes used here and the models selected to represent them are illustrative and by no means exhaustive of the variety of activities embraced by adult education.

The literature also contains curriculum models that are multipurpose and generic. Examples of such models were included in the descriptions in order to reveal the assumptions and developmental activities these robust models require.

All of the curriculum models reflect activity designed to create access to knowledge. The self-directed learning models were included to demonstrate ways in which access is gained, providing a perspective that is too often overlooked in curriculum development.

The descriptions of the curriculum models in the preceding chapters underscore the fact that adult education is made up of a wide variety of educational and training activities. How conceptually convenient it would be if, after becoming familiar with the array of models described in the preceding chapters, certain common threads could be seen to weave through all of the models. That luxury escapes us. The curricular commonplaces of goals, content, method, and evaluation are present in all of the models, but they do not receive similar treatment in each. The ways in which the commonplaces are addressed within each curriculum model depend on a number of factors, not the least of which are the values associated with the purpose or purposes the model is designed to serve. Another factor affecting emphasis on certain commonplaces over others appears to be the excessive reliance some curriculum developers place on behaviorism as the only way to be accountable. In short, there is little evidence of any consistent conceptual scheme, a theory, that would adequately describe and explain the relationships found in the elements of the various curriculum models. Classifying the models according to purpose could make generalizations about the models more refined.

The division of curriculum models according to purpose does not solve all the conceptual problems, but does provide some help in trying to understand the complex field of adult education. Although no single conceptual theme serves to account for all the similarities and differences, the analysis-by-purpose permits some tentative conclusions about adult education curriculum models.

Before proceeding with some tentative conclusions, a note of caution is needed regarding the prescriptive statements found in the literature and how the actual application of the model can be different. It should be obvious that the actual application of any curriclum model can be different from the portrayal of the model in the literature. Minor differences, in fact, are anticipated by most of the model developers—they consistently advise that specific, "real-life" situations may dictate somewhat different decisions from those the model suggests. Local adaptations are assumed, then, to be givens. The differences among the curriculum models described in the preceding chapters and below are differences that are likely to be natural extensions of the models' purposes and not artifacts of a specific application.

The Effects of Purpose

The purpose an activity serves can affect all other aspects of that activity. The curricular commonplaces of goals, content, method, and evaluation and the degree to which learners contribute to decisions about them, can be influenced by the purpose the curriculum model is designed to serve.

The decisions about goals, content, method, and evaluation within the organizational effectiveness models described in Chapters 1 and 2 are driven by the organization, in the form of a specific employer or a specific job. The models may provide opportunities for learners to contribute to the decisions of content and method, but ultimately the needs of the organization or job will determine the final outcome. The emphasis of both models is on learners' terminal behaviors that match those required by the organization or job. Both of these models can be considered institutional models because of the pervasive effect the organization has on them.

Liberal education models, as described in Chapters 3 and 4, may permit learner input in planning the activity but that is overshadowed by the expectation of active learner involvement in the activity itself. The emphasis in all of the liberal education models described is on the process of achieving a liberal education. Terminal behaviors have little utility in liberal education endeavors. The process, usually a discussion format, is essentially all that can be evaluated when adults engage in liberal education activities. The liberal education models defy simple classification.

The literacy models described in Chapters 5 and 6 reveal a more balanced emphasis on both the process of curriculum development and the expected outcomes. The process is critical to helping the learner feel empowered to learn and the outcome, the ability to read, is quite unambiguous. Empowerment is accomplished in both models by using the learner's experience as a bridge between the known and the unknown. Newman's model of literacy includes special attention to the learner's interests. The interest inventory she recommends using serves as a point of departure for planning specific lessons, thus legitimating the learner's experiences as contributive to the learning process. When the teacher acknowledges the learner's experiences and interests by making them integral elements of what is to be learned, the undertaking serves as an example of a cooperative curriculum model.

Freire's literacy model has both an individual and social focus and is a cooperative one in the same manner as Newman's. Freire's assumptions about purpose and approach are made more explicit than Newman's, and have obvious political implications, but his overall design can be viewed as essentially cooperative because it relies heavily on the adults' willingness to participate.

A greater number of variables become evident when considering the continuing professional education models described in Chapters 7 and 8. Three different models would be necessary to accommodate the three modes of learning Houle observed in the professionalizing occupations he studied. Instruction, inquiry, and performance would have to be planned around different purposes and consequently different models would be appropriate.

The American Nurses' Association's standards and guidelines, described in Chapter 8, address two learning modes: instruction and inquiry. The guidelines they suggest for inquiry, however, because they emphasize predetermined, behavioral objectives, were seen to be more appropriate for instruction than inquiry.

The multipurpose and generic models are difficult to generalize about with regard to purpose because specific applications can take many different forms. The particular form of these models could be analyzed in terms of the primary purpose the activity is serving and how this purpose may be affecting the decisions about goals, content, method, and evaluation.

The descriptions of self-directed learning that appear in Chapters 10 and 11 reveal what may be the single most important variable associated with any of the curriculum models. Self-directed learning, by definition, is an activity in which the learner has control over the variables associated with the learning project. Learner control is the preeminent feature of self-directed learning and this control, or the lack of it, may be a useful way to analyze all curriculum models. Schroeder (1980), for example, has devised a method for quantitatively assessing agent and client control over decisions associated with a designed learning activity. But simple quantification is not enough, as a discussion of participation in single purpose models will reveal.

Participation and Purpose

Unlike conventional K-12 schooling where participation is considered as a constant, the field of adult education has to consider participation as a variable, dependent on a number of factors. The relationship of participation to purpose, although not always a direct one, can be seen in the descriptions of the single purpose models.

Voluntary participation, as mentioned in the Introduction, is considered a basic principle or even an integral part of the definition of adult education. Ideally, adults choose to participate in educational or training activities when they perceive a congruence between the purpose of the activity and their own needs or interests. The emphasis in the preceding sentence is on the word choose. Simple congruence between purpose and needs or interests is overshadowed if individuals think they are being coerced to participate or not given any latitude to legitimately decline to participate. The significance of being treated like an object is likely to supersede the feeling of being in concert with the activity's purpose, goals, etc. It is also possible that if an individual expects to have an influence over choice of content or method and discovers those decisions are "off-limits" to learners, the effect could be more pervasive than realizing needs and interests were perfectly accommodated. All of which is to say that while being mindful of the purpose being served is critical to understanding and planning an educational or training activity, purpose alone is not the only consideration that may be important to the adult learner.

Voluntary participation is indispensable to the success of the liberal education and literacy models. Unless potential learners are in a situation where an academic degree or certificate of achievement is required for continued employment or promotion, the adults who participate in liberal education and literacy programs do so on their own volition. Potential learners may expect to be told exactly what the content and methods will be or they may expect to be included in decisions about content and method. Purpose, however is nonnegotiable: it is a form of self-improvement.

Content and method are predetermined in the Great Books discussion groups, but the other three liberal education models described in Chapters 3 and 4 contain some provisions for learners to help in planning content and method. The decisions are open to learners in the other models ostensibly to incorporate individual learning preferences, which, in turn, would likely enhance the probability of continued participation. Having learners help decide content and method is not to be construed as crass expediency to sustained participation, but as a legitimate appeal to most adults' interest in being considered as partners in a learning venture. Within the literacy models described in Chapters 5 and 6 the involvement of learners is absolutely critical to their learning to read. In addition, in Freire's model, the inclusion of the learners is essential to the philosophical underpinnings of the entire model. The learners have to be involved if they are to be subjects and not objects of educational activities.

In contrast to the liberal education and literacy models, the curriculum models used to achieve organizational effectiveness described in Chapters 1 and 2 reveal an aura of coercion about them. The Critical Events Model described in Chapter 1 exists solely to satisfy an organizational need. Not all such needs are in conflict with personal needs, but if the difference between meeting organizational and personal needs is to be negotiated; the organization, by definition, will take precedence in whatever compromise is achieved.

The vocational-technical, competency-based model described in Chapter 2 focuses on specific competencies required for specific jobs. Coercion to participate in such training operates only to the extent that this type of training is perceived by the learners as necessary to being employed or promoted. Jobs are determined by organizations, hence training for jobs is training for organizational effectiveness. No one needs to be apologetic about the relationship between training and organizational effectiveness. What is needed, however, is the realization that whatever personal needs and interests a learner brings to the training situation are likely to receive less (if any) attention than the task at hand, i.e., achieving organizational effectiveness.

Competency-based curriculum models have another, perhaps equally important, aura about them that has to do with their specificity of results. The vocational-technical model described in Chapter 2 exudes an explicitness of goals and objectives that is in stark contrast to the liberal education models. And a similar contrast is evident when comparing the competency-based model to the two literacy models, each of which includes a great deal of attention to the learner's interests and attitudes. The competency-based model attends almost exclusively to results, stated as unambiguously as possible. The adult students who know what they want may well appreciate the no-nonsense, results-oriented approach of the competency-based model. This allure of accountability of competency-based models cannot be denied. To what extent this type of model may have to be supplemented with others that attend to interests and attitudes of learners, the "whole" adult, is a question that may relate to participation in programs built around competency-based curriculum models.

Continuing professional education, described in Chapters 7 and 8, can be seen to serve both professional and organizational needs. The extent to which CPE fulfills an individual's interests will depend on the extent to which the individual identifies with a particular organization or professionalizing occupation. If the goals of an organization are internalized by individuals, they will be more likely to participate willingly in the CPE activity—likewise with regard to the goals of a professionalizing occupation. As in the case of organizational effectiveness described earlier, the potential learners are expected to reconcile their own goals with those of the organization in which they work and/or the professionalizing occupation of which they are members.

Multipurpose and Generic Models

The multipurpose model described in Chapter 9 revealed a broadly based (macro) conception of education that could make an impact on an entire social system or subsystem. The primary emphasis was on identifying and mobilizing members of the targeted social system who had sufficient power to contribute to the variety of purposes the model can accommodate. Being multipurpose, the model can serve a variety of needs, which is exactly what the Cooperative Extension Service is about. A more detailed analysis of this multipurpose model would depend on the specific purpose being served by a particular activity.

The generic models described in Chapters 12 and 13 represent ambitious attempts to provide generalizations about creating, and in Houle's one case of individual effort, gaining, access to knowledge. Houle's structural/functional approach to educational design is the more comprehensive of the two described here, and probably the most comprehensive of all. His contention, however, that any design is a complex of interacting elements and not necessarily a sequence of events, stymies the uninitiated who frequently are searching for a rational order to the "creative anarchy" of adult education. Houle, of course, is right. The propensity the uninitiated and some experienced educators have for looking for a rational order in something as complex as education has to be tempered with the realization that educators are working with unpredictable people, who defy simple analysis, and are not always accommodated by a model that reduces all outcomes to specific, predetermined behaviors.

Boone's generic model is institutionally based, but addresses the typical shortcoming of such models by including a staff development component. The purpose of the staff development is to remain mindful of and responsive to the changing needs of the clients served by the institution. Boone's model, however, like Verduin's (1980) before him, relies so much on behaviorism in terms of objectives and evaluation that it is rendered less useful than intended. Boone's and Houle's generic models, because of their thoroughness with respect to detail often overlooked in other models, can supply checklists for planning an educational or training activity.

Alternative Approaches

Alternative approaches to understanding more about curriculum models of adult education could take other forms. The national study of urban public school ABE programs conducted by Mezirow et al. (1975) is an example of an effort to make more accurate generalizations about actual practices. Both qualitative and quantitative descriptions of urban public school ABE programs during the early 1970s are presented in their book, *Last Gamble on Education* (1975). If other studies, equally broad in scope and carefully conducted, were made of organizational effectiveness, liberal education, and continuing professional education endeavors, perhaps more insight could be gained about different adult education curriculum models. The models, after all, speak primarily to intention whereas actual programs represent function and effect. The difference between intention and effect is what Goodlad (1979) calls slippage. The difference also could be considered the "hidden curriculum." Until more descriptive studies are made, however, relatively little will be known about the differences.

Another approach is the biographical, epitomized by Houle's *Patterns of Learning* (1984). His study of life-span education experienced by Thoreau, Everett, Graham, and others represents a rich source of specific (ideographic) analysis that permits the beginning of generalizations across various individuals and settings (nomothetic analysis). Houle's approach is reminiscent of, but more instructive than, Mailer's *Armies of the Night: History as a Novel/The Novel as History* (1968). If other biographies could be studied, a more qualitative source of information would be available to adult educators interested in planning for lifelong learning.

A collection of actual program descriptions that illustrate the application of andragogy—the art and science of helping adults learn—is present in Knowles and associates' *Andragogy in Action* (1984). They provide information about programs that seek to embrace the principles of andragogy in different settings. Perhaps more such descriptions will provide a critical mass of literature that reveals a conceptual clarity not yet present in all models.

Overview of Models

The most common formal curriculum model has been variously called: institutional; classical; Tylerian; and rational. The model, whatever its name, is assumed to have certain characteristics, sufficient to differentiate it from other models. But does it? If a liberal education purpose is being served by an institution, it appears as if the purpose above all will have a greater impact on curriculum development decisions than anything inherent in the model itself. Organizational effectiveness typically is served by an institutional model, as well, but curricular decisions will be affected more by the purpose than the particular process of the model. Purpose will drive the decisions, not exclusively, but predominantly.

If curriculum developers continue to treat the institutional model as if it were a Procrustean bed, curriculum development in the future is not likely to be much different from the 1920s, when the model was first delineated. (Pratt, 1980) By focusing on the purpose, however, it may be that other models will emerge that are more consistent with purpose than what appears to be present to date.

The cooperative or collaborative model typically is not institutionally based and always requires active involvement from the learner for its success. This model may be considered an extension of the self-directed learning model wherein the learner cedes some control of the variables associated with gaining access to knowledge. The encounter between facilitator and learner may not be "of equals" literally, as some would suggest, but it could be likened to Cousins' account of the relationship between medical doctor and patient: "The most valuable service a physician can provide to a patient is helping him to maximize his own recuperative and healing potentialities" (1979, p. 139). The allusion to a therapy model can be overdone, as Houle (1972) warns, but similarities in the nature of the relationship cannot be denied. Nothing in Cousins' portrayal of the physician-patient encounter negates the knowledge and training of the former, but it does elevate the patient to something other than an object. Whether or not adult educators can create access to knowledge or facilitate gaining such access without treating learners as objects remains to be seen.

No single curriculum model can adequately account for the many adult education activities described in the preceding chapters. Houle's generic approach (1972) affirmed the notion that a dynamic system and not a static taxonomy is what is needed to understand better the planning for adult education activities. To seek one comprehensive model to account for all that is considered curriculum development in adult education would be an imprudent proposition. But to consider all curriculum development to be situation specific would be equally imprudent. A middle position between these two extremes can be reached and some ambiguity can be removed if planners and participants are more aware of purpose. Planning for adult education cannot be reduced to one simple maxim. And it was never intended here to reveal easy explanations for the myriad relationships in any educational or training endeavor. The persistent problems associated with curriculum, and adult education generally, will remain.

Becoming aware of the various ways access to knowledge is created for adults is one way to become aware of the myriad activities that constitute adult education. And the curriculum models can be useful guides in developing curricula. More enlightened decisions about goals, content, methods, and evaluation, however, will be more likely when planners and participants are mindful of purpose.

References

Adler, M. J. 1982. *The Paideia Proposal.* New York: Macmillan.

Adler, M. J. 1983. *Paideia Problems and Possibilities.* New York: Macmillan.

Adler, M. J. 1984. *The Paideia Program: An Educational Syllabus.* New York: Macmillan.

Adler, M. J. and C. Van Doren. 1984. "The Conduct of Seminars," in M. J. Adler, 1984.

American Nurses' Association. 1978. *Continuing Education in Nursing: Guidelines for Staff Development.* Kansas City: American Nurses' Association.

American Nurses' Association. 1978. *Self-Directed Continuing Education in Nursing.* Kansas City: American Nurses' Association.

American Nurses' Association. 1979. *Continuing Education in Nursing An Overview.* Kansas City: American Nurses' Association.

American Nurses' Association. 1984. *Standards for Continuing Education in Nuring.* Kansas City: American Nurses' Association.

Apple, M. 1979. *Ideology and Curriculum.* London: Routledge and Kegan Paul.

Apple, M. and L. Weiss. 1983. *Ideology and Practice in Schooling.* Philadelphia: Temple University Press.

Apps, J. W. 1985. *Improving Practice in Continuing Education.* San Francisco: Jossey-Bass.

Ashton-Warner, S. 1963. *Teacher.* New York: Simon and Schuster.

Beal, G. M., R. C. Blount, R. C. Powers, and W. J. Johnson. 1966. *Social Action and Interaction in Program Planning* Ames: Iowa State University Press.

Bee, B. 1981. "The Politics of Literacy," in R. Mackie, ed. *Literacy and Revolution: The Pedagogy of Paulo Freire.* New York: Continuum.

Blank, W. E. 1982. *Handbook for Developing Competency-Based Training Progams.* Englewood Cliffs: Prentice-Hall, Inc.

Bloom B. S. 1981. *All Our Children Learning: A Primer for Parents, Teachers, and Other Educators.* New York: McGraw-Hill.

Bobbitt, F. 1924. *How to Make a Curriculum.* Boston: Houghton Mifflin Co.

Boone, E. J. 1985. *Developing Programs in Adult Education.* Englewood Cliffs: Prentice-Hall.

Boyd, W. (trans. & ed.). 1956. *The Emile of Jean Jacques Rousseau.* New York: Teachers College Press.

Boyd, R. D., J. W. Apps, and Associates. 1980. *Redefining the Discipline of Adult Education.* San Francisco: Jossey-Bass.

Brookfield, S.D. 1985. "Analyzing a Critical Paradigm of Self-Directed Learning: A Response." *Adult Education Quarterly,* 36 (1), 60–64.

Brookfield, S. D. 1986. *Understanding and Facilitating Adult Learning.* San Francisco: Jossey-Bass.

220   Curriculum Models in Adult Education

Charters, W. W. 1923. *Curriculum Construction*. New York: The Macmillan Co.
Clark, K. M. 1986. "Recent Developments in Self-Directed Learning." *The Journal of Continuing Education in Nursing*, 17 (3), 76–80.
College of Liberal Studies. 1985. *Bulletin, 1985-86*. Norman: University of Oklahoma.
Cousins, N. 1979. *Anatomy of an Illness as Perceived by the Patient: Reflections on Healing and Regeneration*. New York: W. W. Norton.
Darkenwald, G. G. and S. B. Merriam. 1982. *Adult Education: Foundations of Practice*. New York: Harper and Row.
Freire, P. 1970. *Pedagogy of the Oppressed*. New York: Herder and Herder.
Freire, P. 1985. *The Politics of Education: Culture, Power, and Liberation*. South Hadley, MA: Bergin and Garvey.
Gagne, R. M. 1965. *The Conditions of Learning*. New York: Holt Rinehart and Winston.
Giroux, H. A. 1983. *Theory and Resistance in Education: A Pedagogy for the Opposition*. South Hadley, MA: Bergin and Garvey.
Goodlad, J. I. and Associates. 1979. *Curriculum Inquiry: The Study of Curriculum Practice*. New York: McGraw-Hill.
Great Books Foundation. 1985. *A Guide for Co-Leaders*. Chicago: The Great Books Foundation.
Griffin, C. 1983. *Curriculum Theory in Adult and Lifelong Education*. London: Croom Helm.
Houle, C. O. 1972. *The Design of Education*. San Francisco: Jossey-Bass.
Houle, C. O. 1980. *Continuing Learning in the Professions*. San Francisco: Jossey-Bass.
Houle, C. O. 1984. *Patterns of Learning: New Perspectives on Life-Span Education*. San Francisco: Jossey-Bass.
Jarvis, P. 1983. *Adult and Continuing Education: Theory and Practice*. London: Croom Helm.
Jarvis, P. 1985. *The Sociology of Adult and Continuing Education*. London: Croom Helm.
Johnstone, J. W. and R. J. Rivera. 1965. *Volunteers for Learning*. Chicago: Adeline.
Joyce, B. R. 1971. "The Curriculum Worker of the Future," in R. McClure, ed. *The Curriculum: Retrospect and Prospect*. Chicago: National Society for the Study of Education.
Knowles, M. S. 1975. *Self-Directed Learning: A Guide for Learners and Teachers*. Chicago: Follett.
Knowles, M. S. and Associates. 1984. *Andragogy in Action: Applying Modern Principles of Adult Learning*. San Francisco: Jossey-Bass.
Kozol, J. 1981. "Foreword," in R. Mackie, ed. *Literacy and Revolution: The Pedagogy of Paulo Freire*. New York: Continuum.
Kozol, J. 1985. *Illiterate America* New York: Anchor Press.
Kreitlow, B. W. and Associates. 1981. *Examining Controversies in Adult Education*. San Francisco: Jossey-Bass.
Lindeman, E. C. 1926. *The Meaning of Adult Education*. New York: New Republic.
Loomis, C. P. 1959. "Toward a Theory of Systematic Social Change," in *Rural Sociology in a Changing Society*. Proceedings of North Central Rural Sociology Committee Seminar. Columbus: Ohio Agricultural Extension Service.
Lyman, H. 1977. *Literacy and the Nation's Libraries*. Chicago: American Library Association.
Mackie, R. ed. 1981. *Literacy and Revolution: The Pedagog of Pualo Freire*. New York: Continuum.
Mager, R. F. 1975. *Preparing Instructional Objectives*. Belmont, CA: Fearon.

Mailer, N. 1968. *Armies of the Night: History as a Novel/The Novel as History*. New York: New American Library.

Malasky, E. W. 1984. "Instructional Strategies: Nonmedia," in L. Nadler, (ed.). *The Handbook of Human Resource Development*. New York: John Wiley and Sons.

McClure, R. M., ed. 1971. *The Curriculum: Retrospect and Prospect*. Chicago: National Society for the Study of Education.

McClure, R. M. 1979. "Institutional Decisions in Curriculum," in J. I. Goodlad and Associates, *Curriculum Inquiry*. New York: McGraw-Hill Book Co.

McGinnis, P. S. C. 1981. "What Should Be the Major Focus of Adult Education?" in B. W. Kreitlow and Associates, *Examining Controversies in Adult Education*. San Francisco: Jossey-Bass.

Mezirow, J., G. G. Darkenwald, and A. B. Knox. 1975. *Last Gamble on Education: Dynamics of Adult Basic Education*. Washington, DC: Adult Education Association of the U.S.A.

Moores, A. and R. Rubin. 1984. *Let's Talk About It: A Planners Manual*. Chicago: American Library Association.

Nadler, L. 1982. *Designing Training Programs*. Reading: Addison-Wesley.

Nadler, L. (ed.). 1984. *The Handbook of Human Resource Development*. New York: John Wiley and Sons.

Newman, A. P. 1980. *Adult Basic Education: Reading*. Boston: Allyn and Bacon.

Peters, J. M. and Associates. 1981. *Building an Effective Adult Education Enterprise*. San Francisco: Jossey-Bass.

Pratt, D. 1980. *Curriculum: Design and Developments*. New York: Harcourt Brace Jovanovich.

Schroeder, W. L. 1981. "Typology of Adult Learning Systems," in J. M. Peters and Associates, *Building an Effective Adult Education Enterprise*. San Francisco: Jossey-Bass.

Schumacker, E. F. 1973. *Small is Beautiful*. New York: Harper and Row.

Sizer, T. R. 1983. "Appendix III," in M. J. Adler, 1983.

Sizer, T. R. 1984. "Coaching," in M. J. Adler, 1984.

Smith, F. B. 1984. "High School Equivalency Preparation for Recent Dropouts," in G. G. Darkenwald and A. B. Knox. *Meeting Educational Needs of Young Adults*. San Francisco: Jossey-Bass.

Sork, T. J. and J. H. Buskey. 1986. "A Descriptive and Evaluative Analysis of Program Planning Literature, 1950–1983." *Adult Education Quarterly*, 32 (2), 86–96.

Squire, J. R. (ed.). 1977. *The Teaching of English: The Seventy-Sixth Yearbook of the National Society for the Study of Education*. Chicago: University of Chicago.

Stubblefield, H. W. 1981. "What Should Be the Major Focus of Adult Education?" in B. W. Kreitlow and Associates. *Examining Controversies in Adult Education*. San Francisco: Jossey-Bass.

Tough, A. 1979. *The Adult's Learning Projects: A Fresh Approach to Theory and Practice in Adult Learning*. Toronto: Ontario Institute for Studies in Education.

Tyler, R. W. 1971. *Basic Principles of Curriculum and Instruction*. Chicago: University of Chicago.

Tyler, R. W. "Instructional Strategies" (Seminar). Department of Adult and Community College Education. North Carolina State University. Raleigh, Feb., 1985, cited in Brookfield, 1986.

Verduin, J. R., Jr. 1980. *Curriculum Building for Adult Learning*. Carbondale: Southern Illinois University Press.

Zais, R. S. 1976. *Curriculum Principles and Foundations*. New York: Thomas Y. Crowell Co.

INDEX

Tests, 89; criterion-referenced, 45;
norm-referenced, 45; performance,
45–47; for use with competency-based
curriculum model, 45–46, 51; written,
46, 47; GED, 79; for diagnosing
reading difficulties, 86
Tough, Allen, 4, 147–61, 163; and
self-directed learning criteria, 150–51
TPO (terminal performance objective),
44, 45
Training, 5, 214; and education
contrasted, 5–6, 34; organizational,
11–54 (*see also* conceptual
programming model); objectives of
organizational, 20; and development

contrasted, 34; generic
vocational-technical, 37–51;
competency-based training technique
contrasted with traditional, 38; and
liberal education contrasted, 53; *see
also* coaching; education
Tyler, R. W., 207
Tyler Rationale, 2

V

Van Doren, C., 60, 61
Verduin, J. R., Jr., 215
V-TECS Consortium, 42, 44